ASIAN CIVILIZATION

This series of interdisciplinary readings is designed to introduce the western reader to the distinctive components of Asian civilization—social order, political institutions, economic problems, and cultural milieu. Each set of paired volumes contrasts ancient and modern subjects; ageless tradition has been balanced by recent analysis to reveal historical continuity amid the unprecedented change occurring in Asia today.

J. Stewart-Robinson, the editor of this volume in the Asian Civilization series, is Associate Professor of Turkish Studies in the Department of Near Eastern Languages and Literatures, University of Michigan, and was Director of the Asian Studies Course there from 1963-65. He is the author of numerous articles and reviews in the field of Near Eastern studies.

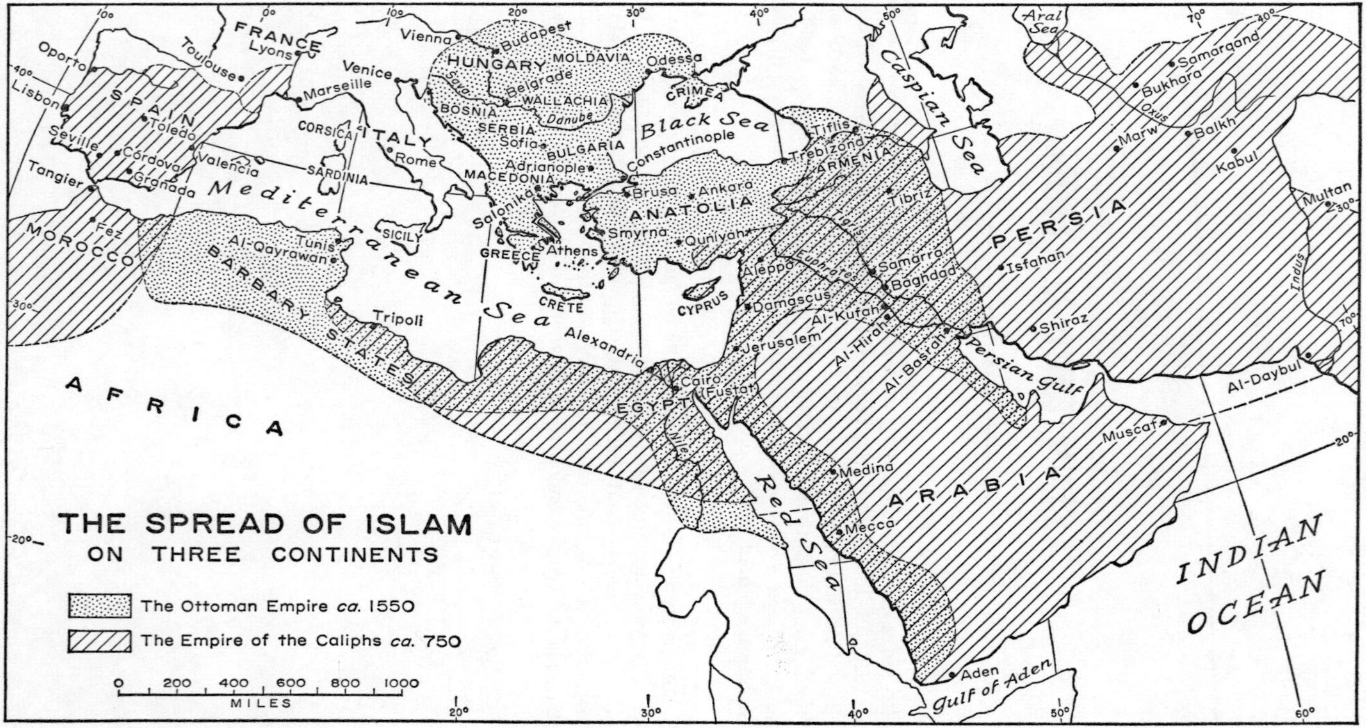
THE SPREAD OF ISLAM
ON THREE CONTINENTS
The Ottoman Empire ca. 1550
The Empire of the Caliphs ca. 750
0 200 400 600 800 1000
MILES
FRANCE
Lyons
Toulouse
Oporto
Lisbon
SPAIN
Toledo
Seville
Córdova
Granada
Valencia
Tangier
Fez
MOROCCO
AFRICA
Marseille
Venice
Vienna
Budapest
HUNGARY
MOLDAVIA
Odessa
CRIMEA
Belgrade
WALLACHIA
Sava
Danube
BOSNIA
SERBIA
Sofia
BULGARIA
Black Sea
Constantinople
CORSICA
ITALY
Rome
SARDINIA
Adrianople
MACEDONIA
Salonika
Mediterranean Sea
SICILY
Tunis
Al-Qayrawan
BARBARY STATES
Tripoli
GREECE
Athens
CRETE
Brusa
Ankara
ANATOLIA
Smyrna
Quniyah
CYPRUS
Alexandria
Cairo
(Fustat)
EGYPT
Nile
Tiflis
Trebizond
ARMENIA
Tibriz
Tigris
Euphrates
Aleppo
Samarra
Baghdad
Damascus
Al-Kufah
Al-Hirah
Jerusalem
Al-Basrah
Persian Gulf
Caspian Sea
Aral Sea
PERSIA
Isfahan
Shiraz
Samarqand
Bukhara
Oxus
Marw
Balkh
Kabul
Multan
Indus
Al-Daybul
Muscat
ARABIA
Medina
Mecca
Red Sea
Aden
Gulf of Aden
INDIAN OCEAN

THE TRADITIONAL NEAR EAST

Edited by

J. Stewart-Robinson

Prentice-Hall, Inc. A SPECTRUM BOOK *Englewood Cliffs, N.J.*

Library of Congress Catalog Card Number: 66-28107.

Printed in the United States of America—C. P92611, C92612

Current printing (last number):

10 9 8 7 6 5 4 3 2 1

CONTENTS

THE TRADITIONAL NEAR EAST

INTRODUCTION

J. Stewart-Robinson

In recent years the Near East has witnessed enormous political and social upheaval, and although the series of "coups" and "counter-coups" that once racked the area has subsided lately, the region is still potentially very explosive. What are the underlying causes of this ever-present tension, and how can the Westerner unfamiliar with the Near East begin to comprehend them? In order for the intelligent layman, as well as the student of Near Eastern affairs, to make an accurate assessment of the situation, he must first acquire a knowledge and understanding of the historical circumstances that brought this situation about. This understanding must be based not only on a knowledge of events and developments since the beginning of what the historians have called the "modern age," but also on sound information concerning the rise, growth, and final form of the traditional Near Eastern societies before their emergence into modern times. Some of the contemporary states of the Near East have hardly begun to change and modernize, and the others, which have succeeded in making that fateful break with the past, are still hampered in their development by vestiges of archaic thinking, outmoded social structures, unviable political modes of behaviors, and anachronisms of all kinds, to say nothing of the persistence, even in this nuclear age, of technologies that in certain areas reach all the way back to the very beginnings of Near Eastern social life. Here the subject becomes clouded, for it is one thing to be able to separate the "modern" from the "traditional" in the Near East of our own generation, and quite another to be able to know exactly what the "traditional" was.

Quite apart from the fact that an understanding of the traditional Near East in and for itself is intrinsically valuable, as heirs to Western civilization we should be aware of the close and long ties of Near Eastern cultures with our own. As the birthplace of the Judaeo-Christian tradition, and as the melting-pot of many other traditions of far-flung provenance that we have indirectly inherited, the Near East constitutes an important element in our own civilization. It therefore behoves us to acquire a broader and deeper knowledge of the area by isolating, identifying, and studying the various ingredients of this society that ultimately went into the making of our own. Since, however, it was in the earlier, or traditional, period rather than in more recent times that the cultural exchange and cross-fertilization between East and West took place, cognizance of at least the principal events and cultural highlights of the traditional Near East is as beneficial as firsthand knowledge of what is actually transpiring in the Near East today. Study of the traditional Near East, therefore, can serve a double-barrelled purpose: to place the present developments in the modern Near East in proper perspective, and to allow us to investigate more meaningfully the roots of our own civilization.

This has been recognized as an acceptable and valid argument by many educators who have striven to create a greater awareness of the importance of exposing our men and women of all academic levels as well as the general public to the need for the study of *all* civilizations. Out of an increased interest in non-European and non-Western cultures and greater concern, in particular, with Asian affairs, there have evolved many and varied programs in our high schools and colleges. With these developments in mind, the readings on the following pages were selected both for the inquisitive general reader with little or no background on the Near East—who will find the selections informative and probably very revealing—and for the student of the Near East—who will easily be able to integrate these readings into his studies and will, in many respects, find in them useful material to complement the courses he takes in any particular discipline.

As far as subject matter is concerned, the eight selections of varying length that follow concentrate on the major characteristics of the Near East as molded almost exclusively by Islam. While not denying the existence of other equally significant faiths in the area, I found it more practical and realistic to present the traditional Near East by way of the obviously predominant one. Geographically, the articles include such areas as the eastern coast of North Africa, the Arabian Peninsula, the Levant, the Persian Gulf area, Iran, Turkistan, Anatolia and, peripherally, the western coast of North Africa, the Iberian Peninsula, and the easternmost parts of Europe. The time period covered ranges from early in the seventh century A.D. to the initial impact of the West upon the Near East late in the eighteenth century, although there are also many references to periods very much earlier and somewhat later.

The selections begin with two admirable articles that set the stage for the discussions that follow. In fact, taken together, the first four pieces in this volume cover the history of the Near East from the rise of Islam in the seventh century A.D. to about the end of the eighteenth century. There is considerable overlapping in subject matter and time covered in the first three of these, but this adds to the value of the articles in that it makes it possible for the reader to look at the facts from three different points of view and at three different sets of circumstances. Professor Gibb's "An Interpretation of Islamic History" and Professor von Grunebaum's "Islam in a Humanistic Education" review more or less the same topics and the same time period (600-1200 A.D.), from the first emergence of Islam as a religion and as the basis of a political and social system to the development, in the later Middle Ages, of an Islamic civilization to its zenith. The former of these two outstanding specialists of Islam seeks to explain the development of the culture by underlining the political and social systems which backed it and by identifying and investigating the forces which acted upon them, while the latter presents the reader with a very skilful sketch of Islam by examining all the areas of human endeavor upon which it has had some influence. Professor Levy's "Persia and the Arabs" emphasizes the contributions of the Persians to the development of Islamic government and culture in the latter part of the same period. The last of the four, Dr. Germanus's "The Role of the Turks in Islam" is much more than an evaluation of the part played by peoples of

Turkish origin in the further spread of the religion and the transformed culture of the bedouins: it is a dated but still reasonably accurate sketch of the history of the Near East and Eastern Europe up to the eve of modern times. Because the modern period in the Near East began when the whole area was under Turkish/Ottoman hegemony, this article serves as a bridge between the truly traditional period covered by the preceding three articles and the modern period treated in a companion Spectrum volume, *The Modern Near East.* Many of the problems which the contemporary Near East faces today date back to the Ottoman period described in Dr. Germanus's article.

The next four pieces treat four specific legal, political, and cultural aspects of the Islamic Near East. While each may be read to great advantage by itself, each is more meaningful if considered in the context of the historical developments treated in the preceding four. Mr. Coulson's "The State and the Individual in Islamic Law" is devoted to a discussion of the relationship of the state and the ruler to canon law, and the rights of the individual vis-à-vis the established theocratic system. The article also dwells on the problems involved in adapting a traditional legal concept to the requirements of modern times, particularly to the concept of guaranteed individual liberties. George Stewart's "Is the Caliph a Pope?" was published at a time when the future of the institution of the Caliphate was a hotly debated topic. Although written more than thirty years ago under circumstances which now no longer obtain, this article will prove instructive to the many students and general readers who inevitably equate the status and functions of the Caliphate with those of the Papacy. Professor Walzer's "The Rise of Islamic Philosophy" was included mainly for two reasons. First, it deals with the thorny problem of Muslim philosophy versus Muslim theology by investigating the works and thinking of two outstanding Muslim philosophers in a manner which even the uninitiated may follow easily. Second, it will bring home to the reader, perhaps more than any of the other articles, the differences and the similarities between Western and Near Eastern thinking, and the indebtedness of the West to the studies and writings of the Muslim philosophers. The selections end with Professor Gabrieli's "Literary Tendencies," a compact review of the Muslim literatures in the three principal languages of the Near East: Arabic, Persian, and Turkish. It is the only authoritative exposition of the unity and variety to be found in this large corpus of literary activity by three contributing languages and peoples that is known to me.

1

AN INTERPRETATION OF ISLAMIC HISTORY

H. A. R. Gibb

I

Islam is a concept which, phenomenalized in a number of linked but diverse political, social, and religious organisms, covers an immense area of space and time. In different regions and epochs it has presented differing features under the impact of and in response to local geographical, social, and political forces. Western Islam for example, in Northwest Africa and medieval Spain, though it was closely related to the Muslim heartlands in Western Asia and its culture was an offshoot from their culture, yet evolved several distinguishing characteristics, some of which in turn influenced Islam in Western Asia. In other large and self-contained geographical areas, such as the Indian subcontinent and Indonesia, or in the steppe-lands extending from southern Russia to the borders of China, parallel factors produced similarly distinguishing forms. Yet each and all of these retain a certain easily recognizable common Islamic stamp. It is impossible within the limits of a single essay to deal with all these diverse regions. The present article is therefore confined to Islam in Western Asia with the double object: (1) of tracing the development of Islamic culture and the gradual evolution which by the end of the fourteenth century [A.D.] had transformed its inner structure, and (2) of examining the processes by which its institutions were moulded into a coherent unity and given their specifically Islamic

Reprinted, with permission, from *The Muslim World,* XLV, 1 (January 1955), 4-15, and XLV, 2 (April 1955), 121-33.

stamp, however widely Islam might spread and however various their external forms. It should thus supply a provisional framework within which (corrected or adjusted where necessary) other studies devoted to particular aspects and relations of Islamic culture may be coordinated.

The rhythms of Islamic history are curiously inverse to those of European history. Both arose from the breakdown of the Mediterranean empire of Rome. While Europe slowly and imperceptibly, and only after several centuries, grew out of the anarchy of the barbarian invasions, Islam suddenly emerged from Arabia and with incredible speed fashioned in less than a century a new imperial structure in Western Asia and the southern and western shores of the Mediterranean. But the contrast goes much deeper. The challenges to the ancient Mediterranean empire and institutions were of two kinds. On the northern borders, the barbarian invaders challenged the Roman political power but entered into its new cultural system, the Catholic Christian Church, and accepted its basic social and religious institutions, upon which ultimately the new European political structures were erected. On the southern and eastern borders, the challenge was not to Roman political power but to the cultural centralization of the Church, and manifested in popular rejection of Catholic orthodoxy in favor of dissident creeds, Donatist, Monophysite, and Nestorian. Islam, after establishing a political system which embraced all these areas of dissidence (together with Persia, which had for centuries maintained against Rome a political struggle backed by a rival religious creed), was confronted with the task of bringing them into a common cultural and religious system, based upon its own universalist concept. To achieve this, it had to counteract, and, as far as possible, extinguish the influence of the earlier universalist concept (Christianity) in Western Asia and the southern half of the Mediterranean, to destroy Zoroastrianism and the other dualist religions of Persia and Mesopotamia, and oppose a barrier to the extension of Buddhism in Central Asia.

The whole of medieval Islamic history is dominated by the effort on the part of the Sunni or "orthodox" religious institution, first, to maintain its universalism against internal and external challenges, and second to realize the widest possible measure of religious, social, and cultural unity throughout the Islamic world. The second of these objects was not achieved until the political unity of Islam had been disrupted, partially re-created, and disrupted again; but in the effort to achieve it a vast area of interaction was created between peoples of diverse stocks and traditions, and in this process—almost, indeed, as a by-product of it—the medieval Islamic culture was brought into existence.

II

The social teaching of Muḥammad was basically a reaffirmation of the ethical ideas common to the monotheistic religions: the brotherhood of all members of the new Islamic Community; their equality [and] intrinsic personal worth in spite of differences of temporal status, function, and wealth; and all the mutual relationships and duties following from these principles, deepened by being stated in terms of inward loyalty and outward obligation to the one God. Furthermore (and this was to prove of fundamental importance for the future development of Islamic culture), it included certain social and ethical obligations—but not the full freedom of brotherhood—towards members of other religious communities, provided that these accepted the political control of the Islamic Community.

As in all religious movements, the concrete social results of this teaching were determined by its impact on the actual historic environment. In Muḥammad's own lifetime, it was received at three different levels. The first was at the level of total conversion, producing religious personalities, whose activities and decisions were motivated by a complete inward acceptance of its spirit and principles. This group, the nucleus of the future religious institution, was in the nature of the case relatively small to begin with but steadily increased with the expansion of the Community. The second was that of formal adhesion, of willing acceptance of the outward prescriptions and duties, without assimilation of their spirit but because of the advantages to be gained by incorporation in the new Community. Its leading representatives were the later Meccan adherents, to whose mercantile temper the external demands of Islam were eminently suited, requiring only the dedication to religious duties of a proportion of time and wealth, and leaving the rest free for personal activities and interest. A further commendation of Islam in Meccan eyes was the firm control which it established over the beduins, whose acceptance was on the third level, that of enforced adherence maintained by threat (and after Muḥammad's death by the application) of military sanctions.

Since, however, inescapable economic forces made any permanent stabilization of inner-Arabian conditions virtually impossible, the mere suppression of beduin opposition—with the implication that the forces of Islam would be used up in an interminable and sterile struggle with the tribesmen—was an inadequate solution for the problem set by them. It was necessary to find the terms on which the tribesmen as a whole could be lifted, if not up to the first level of assimilation, at least on to the level of identifying Islam with their own interests. Hence the trial expeditions deliberately organized by Abū Bakr after Muḥammad's death, when groups of tribesmen were despatched under Meccan commanders towards the frontiers of Syria. The first successes led to a coordinated and organized military campaign which quickly achieved the conquest of the whole country; and the comparative lack of success of the simultaneous campaigns in Iraq under tribal leadership reconciled the tribesmen to a similarly organized campaign under Meccan leadership against the Persian empire, with equally decisive results. The policy of Abū Bakr and his successor 'Umar thus not only achieved their first purpose, of bringing the tribesmen to an enthusiastic acceptance of Islam as the palladium of victory and to unite their forces under commanders appointed by the Caliph, but also a second and not less important result, that the conquests were made with the minimum of disturbance to the economy of the conquered countries and were followed by the rapid establishment of organized central control.

Nevertheless, the material interests of the two main parties to the victory, the tribesmen and the Meccans, were still in opposition to one another. The natural instinct of the tribesmen was to appropriate the conquered lands for their pastures, while the Meccans wished to exploit their resources for their own commercial profit. Although the structure of an agricultural community was unfamiliar to the Arab leaders, they quickly understood its significance as a source of revenue. If it was not to be exposed to injury, the obvious solution was to leave its administration in the hands of the former officials who were familiar with it. While the tribesmen were still engaged in the campaigns and still amenable to the moral authority and control of the Caliphate, they were persuaded to relinquish their claims to the occupation of lands, and to receive in compensation a fixed share of the revenues in monetary stipends and produce. This also enabled the central government to keep the tribesmen concentrated in garrison settlements, instead of spreading in nomadic fashion over the country, and by this means to maintain more effective supervision and control over them.

It was not long, however, before the consciousness of the loss of their independence, combined with the unnatural conditions of life in the garrison cities, generated an increasing violent feeling of resentment amongst the tribesmen, exacerbated by the Meccan exploitation of "their" conquests. The Meccan merchants had not been slow to seize the dazzling prospects opened up by the commerce of Iraq, Syria, and Egypt. They were already active supplying the needs of the new garrison settlements for consumption goods, in forming partnerships with local producers and merchants, and especially in the huge operations of exchange and banking required in the distribution of stipends and transfer to Medina of the fifth of all revenues, and were forming vast commercial establishments manned by slaves and clients. In Medina also, after the first satisfaction with the great increase in wealth and prosperity, there was growing resentment at the rapid affirmation of Meccan political control under the third Caliph, 'Uthmān, and the economic exploitation of the empire.

Open discontent was first expressed by several religious personalities whose conscience was shocked by the worldliness and grasping materialism displayed in the name of Islam. But these only provided a rallying cry and a cloak for the material grievances of the tribesmen and Medinans, who swung into line behind them. The assassination of 'Uthmān by the tribesmen provoked a civil war, in which the religious party at first joined the tribesmen of Iraq, in whom they saw the supporters of the cause of unity on Islamic religious and ethical terms. Opposed to them stood the Meccan Governor of Syria, Mu'āwiya, supported by his tribesmen, more disciplined and sedentarized, and less exposed to exploitation than those of Iraq.

It soon became clear to the religious leaders that the tribal interpretation of Islam carried with it a threat to the whole principle of religious authority and to the system of mutual rights and obligations upon which rested the unity and stability of the Community. The conflict turned out to be one, not between the religious basis and the secular basis of unity, but between unity on modified Meccan terms which at least respected the religious foundations of the Community, and the disruptive forces of tribalism. When the issue was underlined by the emergence in Iraq of the violently sectarian and anti-Meccan group called the Khārijites (*Khawārij*) the choice could not long remain in doubt, and the religious party gradually drifted to the side of Muʻāwiya.

III

The establishment of the Umayyad Caliphate of Damascus ([A.D.] 661) was thus the outcome of a coalition or compromise between those who represented the Islamic ideal of a religious community, united by common allegiance to the heritage of the Prophet, and the Meccan secular interpretation of unity, against the threat of anarchy implicit in tribalism. But this was only a *modus vivendi* reinstating a central authority over the loosely bound provinces of the Arab empire. Three major questions remained to be solved: the relations of the government with the tribes, its relations with the religious party, and the relations between Arabs and non-Arabs in the conquered lands.

In their relations with the tribes, the Umayyad Caliphs at first returned to the old Meccan policy of conciliation by coordinating the interest of the tribesmen with their own, combined with a renewal of the Medinan policy of wars of expansion and distribution of booty. The survival of irreconcilable Khārijite and anti-Umayyad tribal opposition in Iraq stood in the way of their success from the first, and the rapid development of tribal factions forced on them a complete change of policy. The administration was increasingly centralized, and its control tightened over the inner provinces (Iraq, Syria, and Egypt); tribal risings were repressed and Syrian garrisons established to maintain order in Iraq and Persia; most important of all, the tribesmen of Iraq were gradually demilitarized, and were beginning to be absorbed into the new mixed urban societies which were developing in the former garrison cities.

Religious factors entered into this process of centralization on both sides, partly in opposition, but partly also in favoring the growth of an organized central authority. Their awareness of the secular tendencies in the Umayyad house, together with the influence of their religious idealism, inclined the religious leaders in a general way against the Umayyad regime, but their difficulty was to find an alternative that would not disrupt the Community. The excesses of the Khārijites and of the activist Shīʿites discredited them with all but a minority, and an anti-Caliphate set up during a second civil war ([A.D.] 684-91) proved incapable of maintaining order. At the same time the Umayyad Caliphate itself was moving towards the universalist Islamic view, as the religious and ethical principles of Islam percolated in the course of the century more deeply into Arab society and affected its outlook and principles of conduct. The outcome of this symbiosis was the emergence of a semi-official interpretation of Islam, supported by a considerable body of religious opinion, and it is noteworthy that the first condemnations for heresy took place under the later Umayyad Caliphs.

By the end of the first century,* however, non-Arabs were beginning to enter the ranks of religious teachers in growing numbers. These naturally accepted Islam in its most universalist interpretation, without any qualifying admixture of Arab ideas; as they were emotionally opposed to the Umayyads because of the grievances and social inferiority of the non-Arabs, they rejected the conformist attitude of the Umayyad supporters, as well as the other Arab sectarian interpretations, and remained on the whole on the neutral ground of doctrinal rigorism.

The most difficult problem for the Umayyads was to integrate the social structure of the Arab state as organized after the conquests with the agricultural economy of the conquered provinces, and to do so in a manner consistent with the ethical principles of Islam. What gave the problem a peculiar intensity was the movement of conversion to Islam among both landowners and cultivators, who continued nevertheless to suffer from their former social and eco-

* Anno Hegira, Islamic Calendar dated from A.D. 622, which is the year of Muḥammad's flight from Mecca to Medina [Ed.].

nomic disabilities. It was eventually solved towards the end of the Umayyad period (but only after bitter struggles) by assimilating new Arab landowners to non-Arab landowners, and by exempting converted cultivators from the poll-tax payable by all non-Muslim subjects. Both measures led towards an assimilation of Arabs and Muslim non-Arabs, and at the same time towards uniformity of administrative practice in the Arab empire; but they came too late to check the accumulated sense of grievance against Umayyad rule, which in the eyes of the developing "religious institution" stood for the political domination and social privilege of the Arabs. Both activist and neutralist religious oppositions joined with a revolt of the Yemen faction of tribesmen to bring down the Umayyad Caliphate ([A.D.] 750); and thus, after having (in alliance with the Umayyads) dissociated the religious polity of Islam from the extreme sectarian and fanatical interpretations of the Khārijites and the ultra-Shī'tes, now also publicly dissociated it from concept of Arab predominance.

IV

The new 'Abbāsid line of Caliphs, although themselves, as relatives of the Prophet, also of Meccan Arab origin, clearly recognized the importance which the religious leaders had assumed in the framework of the empire, and made it one of the cornerstones of their policy to associate them with the new regime. The evolution which had begun under the Umayyads towards centralized monarchical institutions and the merging of the hitherto privileged Arabs into the general Muslim population would have continued in any case, but it was accelerated and given a more definite direction by the fact that the dynasty was brought to power and maintained in it by an alliance of the Arab colonists and Islamized Persian aristocracy of Khūrasān. The increasing employment of non-Arabs in the administration favored the revival of the old Sassanian court ceremonial and administrative traditions, while the constitution of a Khurasanian standing army freed the monarchy from the pressures of the Arab tribal structure. The Arab landowners were integrated in the Persian feudal system, and the expansion of industry, commerce, and material and intellectual culture in Iraq and Persia brought Arabs and non-Arabs together in social, economic and intellectual activities.

The religious policy of the 'Abbāsids also was affected by the same influences. They not only placed a new emphasis on the religious status and functions of the Caliphate, and by their patronage of the religious leaders gave an impulse to the propagation of an "official orthodoxy," but also, on lines reminiscent of the Sassanid Zoroastrian organization, began to centralize the religious institutions under state control.

In all these developments, however, there were implicit certain dangers for the principle of Islamic universalism, the maintenance of the unity of the Muslim Community in its religious and ethical attitudes by acknowledgment of one common authority, although at first sight it might seem to be favored by the establishment of the universal empire of the 'Abbāsids. The rapid social and economic development in Iraq and Persia was not paralleled in Syria and the African provinces, where the Arab tribal structure persisted with little change, and the solutions to the problems of faith and order worked out in the former might be inapplicable to or even rejected by the latter. Still more, too close an association of orthodoxy with the 'Abbāsid Caliphate might well lead, and did in fact lead, to the rejection of orthodoxy by sections politically opposed to 'Abbāsid rule, as in the adhesion of the Berber opposition in Northwest Africa to Khārijism and the increasing attraction of the Arab tribesmen in Arabia and the Syrian desert to Shī'ism. The dangers could not be averted by maintenance of 'Abbāsid political authority by force, but only if religious authority were clearly distinguished from political authority and if necessary in opposition to it.

The problem was probably not at first explicit to the religious leaders in these terms, but it is a proof of the vitality of the Islamic religious impulse that their activities tended, even if unconsciously, in this direction. Although they accepted on the whole the 'Abbāsid "official interpretation" for some seventy or eighty years, and supported the measures employed by the state for religious unification and against heresy, yet there was from the first a current of opposition to some of its manifestations and to State control of religious functions, and an insistence of the free personal responsibility of the religious teacher. The conflict was brought into the open by the attempt of the Caliph Al-Ma'mūn and his successors to impose the Hellenizing doctrines of the group of religious teachers known as the Mu'tazila as the "official interpretation," and their persecution of the leaders of the opposing orthodox school. The struggle ended with the victory of the orthodox, and proved once and for all that the religious institution of Islam was independent of the Caliphate or any other political institution, that its sources of authority could not be controlled by political governors but were possessed by the Community in its own right, and that the Caliphate itself was only an emanation of that authority and its political symbol.

This episode was fundamental for the whole future of Islam in freeing it from identification with any political regime, and allowing the religious institution, and the Community with it, freedom to develop along the lines of its own inner logic and temperament. But simultaneously—in a more complex and less explicit manner—the conflict, between the religious and political institutions was being fought out on another field, and this time with a less favorable outcome for the religious institution.

The introduction of the Persian monarchical tradition and political philosophy into the Muslim State resulted in a conflict of social and ethical ideals, which was fought out largely in a "battle of the books." The Persianizing movement, known as the *Shu'ūbīya* movement, is usually regarded as a current reaction among the Persians against Arab dominance. But this is too narrow an interpretation. Its representatives were the class of secretaries in government service, whose influence had greatly increased under the 'Abbāsid Caliphs owing to the rapid expansion of the bureaucracy and the growing power of viziers and heads of administrative departments (*dīwāns*). From late Umayyad times the secretaries had found their models in the court literature of Sassanian Persia, and the significance of the Shu'ūbīya movement is that it represents the efforts of the secretarial class (while avoiding open conflict with the religious institution) not only to establish the dominance of the Persian tradition at the court, but to revive the old Persian social structure with its rigid class divisions, and to substitute the spirit of Persian culture for the surviving influences of the Arab tradition in the new and rapidly developing urban society in Iraq, by the spread of translations and popular works of Persian origin.

Its first effects were to encourage the revival of the latent Manichaeism in Iraq, and the spread, in much wider circles, of religious indifference or concealed disrespect for Islam. While the official institution tried to stamp out heresy by persecution, the more advanced and rigorous group of the religious leaders, known as the Mu'tazila, sought and found in Greek philosophical literature and Christian-Hellenistic apologetic works the dialectic equipment to meet and overcome the dualist arguments and to reinforce an ethic based on the Qur'ān. At the same time, as the Shu'ūbīya movement passed into a phase of open attack on the Arabs and sarcastic criticism of Arab traditions and pretensions, it brought the whole body of the religious institution up in defense of Arabic studies on religious grounds, since it was these studies which supplied the basis of the developing "religious sciences." Out of the effort to counteract the literary activities of the Shu'ūbīs, a new Arabic humane literature was born, steeped in the traditions and institutions of Arabia, both before and after the rise of Islam; and the force and weight of the double counter-attack quickly checked the dangers implicit in the Shu'ūbīya movement.

By this victory the Islamic religious institution, which had already rejected any domination of its ideals of faith and order by Arab social traditions, now equally rejected the Persian interpretation of Islam as a state-religion and the dominance of Persian social traditions. But the victory was bought at a price. On the one hand the link between the religious sciences and Arabic philology had now been expanded into something not far from identification of the religious culture of Islam with the Arabic humanities. It is a strange phenomenon that while Islam began as a protest against Arab culture and tradition as a whole, by the end of this period the literary heritage of ancient Arabia was indissolubly linked up with Islam, to be carried with it to the ends of the old world. On the other hand, the influence of the secretarial class had been strong enough to force a measure of compromise. Several of the principal elements of the Sassanian tradition were incorporated in the literature of the Arabic humanities, and acquired an established and permanent place in Islamic culture in relation to the principles of government, in spite of their conflict with its inner spirit.

This concession was highly characteristic of an orthodox religious institution, which while standing fast on the principle of its spiritual independence and its right and duty to assert Islamic ethical standards, yet recognized the facts of the actual situation and the dangers of an excessive rigidity to the maintenance of unity. At the same time, by admitting this discordant element into the general fabric of Islamic culture, it brought a kernel of derangement into Muslim society. Its immediate effect was to bring to the surface the hitherto latent or concealed division between the religious institution and the ruling institution, and to set the latter free to pursue its own course of development with relatively little control from the side of the religious institution; ultimately, as it diverged more and more widely from the ethical standards of Islam, the orthodox *'ulamā'* themselves were to find their spiritual independence endangered by the further concessions and compromises wrung from them for the sake of the principle of unity.

V

The process analyzed in the preceding sections, by which the orthodox religious leaders disentangled Islam from political and racial interests and traditions, involved a parallel and simultaneous process of definition of its content. Islam was at first an orientation of life in all its aspects in a particular ethical direction, dictated by the acceptance of certain general beliefs on the authority of Quranic revelation. In the early struggles, the religious leaders aimed to maintain that orientation against a variety of challenges, external in the sense that their motivating forces were derived from other systems of values, though issuing from within the Community and expressed in terms of a particular interpretation of Islam. In meeting each challenge, therefore, they were compelled to oppose its particular interpretation, but their tendency was at first to reject what was opposed rather than assert positively what was to be accepted, and thus maintain the widest possible measure of moral unity. This policy, consciously and consistently pursued, became a marked characteristic of orthodoxy; unlike the fissiparous and exclusive groups which upheld the rejected doctrines, its leaders were unwilling to draw hard and fast lines (beyond the simplest test of adherence to the Community) and tolerated a considerable degree of freedom of interpretation and even divergence in external institutions.

With the development of the religious organization and the advance from defense against deviation to positive definition of doctrine, involving the creation of a theological science, a step of decisive importance was taken for the whole history of Islam.[1] For this was its first intellectual adventure; it absorbed the energies of most of its intellectual leaders in the second, third, and fourth centuries [A.H.], and consequently gave a permanent bias to Islamic intellectual culture.

The origins of its methodology are to be found in the practical problems with which the Community was confronted rather than in any philosophical tendencies. Although the authority of the Qur'ān was absolute and unchallenged, the development of doctrine and law from its religious and ethical contents involved a process of elucidation and interpretation. The first problem appears to have arisen in regard to the application of law. By the end of the first century [A.H.], separate and diverging rules of law were being applied in different cities and provinces, based on the independent interpretations of local teachers, and complicated by survivals of customary law and administrative regulations. The religious leaders saw in this a danger, especially when local rules appeared to diverge from the ethical principles of the Qur'ān. The method by which they proceeded was to produce "traditions" from contemporaries of the Prophet which related the decisions of Muḥammad on specific points, and to claim for these binding authority scarcely inferior to that of the Qur'ān. Although at first the authenticity of many Traditions was disputed by the jurists, and much confusion was caused by the production of contradictory Traditions, the strength of religious feeling behind the movement ultimately forced a general acceptance of the principle.[2] This in turn involved the elaboration of a new science, whose objects were the collection, criticism, classification, and coordination of Traditions, and the attainment as far as possible of an agreed and generally accepted corpus. This task

[1] For an analysis of this process see A. J. Wensinck, *The Muslim Creed,* Cambridge, 1932.

[2] This development is studied more particularly in J. Schacht, *The Origins of Muhammadan Jurisprudence,* Oxford, 1950.

absorbed much of the energies of religious and legal scholars in the third century [A.H.], and was achieved with such success that henceforward the Tradition of the Prophet ranked as a second authoritative source of law and doctrine.

The same method was then applied to dogmatic theology, in the conflict with the speculative reasoning applied by the Mu'tazilite school to the interpretation of Quranic doctrine. The orthodox leaders proceeded not so much by argument as by production of Prophetic Traditions in support of their positions, and in the same way swung the main body of Muslims into line behind them. There can be little doubt, however, that the classical collections of Prophetic Traditions made in the third century [A.H.] do substantially represent the views of the general body of orthodox religious teachers of the first three or four generations, and it is almost as certain that the views expressed in them faithfully reflect the teachings and ethical attitudes of the Qur'ān.

The Muslim doctors who elaborated this defense of unity against disruptive deviations were still aware of its artificial foundations, and the techniques of study included in the "sciences of Tradition" were designed to authenticate the whole structure by a system of formal criteria. But this was not enough. In conformity with the general trend of Sunnī thought, the foundations were underpinned by the principle that once agreement on any main issue of doctrine of law had been reached by responsible scholars, it was final and conclusive, and to reopen controversy on it was heresy. On lesser matters, diversity of opinion and practice was permissible. By this principle the orthodox institution was enabled, in spite of the absence of any formal organization, to hold together in all later centuries, and to remain essentially one in the face of political pressures, calamities, and the influx of new ideas and peoples.

On the other hand it was this combination of (1) a God-given and unchallengeable sacred book, interpreted and supplemented by (2) an artificial creation of Prophetic Tradition, itself canonized by (3) the doctrine of consensus (*ijmā'*), and thereby excluded from any but formal study by predetermined methods and rules, which established the basic character and attitudes of Muslim theological studies, however widely the range of theological discussion might extend in the future. By confining scholarship within the limits of a body of accepted teaching, it gradually diminished and finally inhibited the independent examination of authorities, sources, and methods, and condemned it more and more to mere transmission of the known and given, and the elaboration of subsidiary detail in commentary and super-commentary. The habit of transmission of what had been accepted on authority, inculcated first in the sciences of law and theology, ultimately extended its influence over all Muslim studies in every field of learning, to the exclusion of personal investigation.

But these results were not immediate. The first systems to become crystallized were in the field of orthodox law (*Sharī'ah*), and the importance of this early and relatively rapid stabilization of legal norms, with their effects upon the social ethics of the Community will be seen later. In dogmatics, however, while universal agreement had been reached by the end of the third century [A.H.] on fundamentals, principles, and authorities, there was still room for variety in interpretation. This was of great significance in the history of Islamic culture. For although there were currents of rigorism in some of these interpretations, the majority of orthodox leaders continued to admit a certain range of individual freedom. Thus they not only gave room for the development of cultural and intellectual activities which found expression in the "Islamic Renaissance" of the fourth, fifth, and sixth centuries [A.H.], but themselves participated in them in a certain measure.

VI

The credit for the "Renaissance" itself, however, is not to be given solely to the toleration of the orthodox institution. Even in its intellectual and religious aspects, much of it was due in a positive sense to unorthodox and sectarian influences, and to the widespread growth of material culture resulting from economic development and prosperity. These also, during the preceding centuries, had been developing independently of the orthodox religious culture; and at the time when they came to fruition, in the fourth century A.H., the orthodox were the less able to control their intellectual or material activities because, from the fourth to the middle of the fifth century, almost the whole of the central Islamic lands were governed by Shī'ite princes.

There may be a certain causal relation between these facts and a very remarkable feature of the Islamic Renaissance: the personal and individual character of most of its cultural achievements. Orthodoxy from the first stressed the "collectivity" as against the individual; even the individual personalities who played a leading part in the evolution of the religious institution were more often representatives of collective tendencies than creative thinkers. The great biographical dictionaries of orthodox scholars are concerned very little with their individuality as persons, but only with their contributions to the transmission of the collective heritage. It is a tempting conclusion that it was the other currents of intellectual activity, outside the orthodox institution, which were mainly responsible for the appearance and activity of those individuals whose personal contributions swelled the total of achievements of medieval Islamic culture, even when they themselves were orthodox.

It may be surprising, at first sight, that many of the most active movements and personalities in the third and fourth centuries [A.H.] have Shīʿite attachments, since Shīʿism in its organized dogmatic institution is even more authoritarian than orthodoxy. But Shīʿism at this time was more of a widely diffused emotional or intellectual tendency, sometimes combined with Sunnī orthodoxy, and it is erroneous to visualize hard and fast lines of sectarian division as already solidified in the fourth century. It was natural that individuals who were emotionally or intellectually opposed to the developing tendencies within orthodoxy should find more freedom in the looser and vaguer current of Shīʿism. Moreover, although the orthodox institution had asserted its spiritual independence of the political institution, it still continued to be associated with the civil authorities, partly because of its horror of disunity, and partly owing to the government's control of religious patronage. For similar reasons, the bureaucracy and the feudal landowners were, as a whole, strongly orthodox, and thus the leaders of orthodoxy not only were classed, but classed themselves, among the élite (*al-khāṣṣat*), in contradistinction to the merchants, troops, artisans, peasants, and nomads (*al-ʿawāmm*). Many religious leaders and teachers, as will be seen later, were embarrassed or dissatisfied with this situation, and while their strong feeling for the cohesion of the Community kept most of them loyal to orthodoxy, the more extreme or more independent were liable to be attracted into one or other of the opposition movements.

The phenomenal expansion of industry and commerce had in the meantime created a network of cities in the eastern provinces, with a highly developed urban life and prosperous merchant communities, possessing knowledge of the world, intelligence, boldness, and independence. Their interests (as usual in flourishing commercial civilizations) were mainly secular, even while they remained attached to orthodoxy; but they no longer found adequate intellectual nourishment in Persian romances or the classical Arab humanities. With the political unification of Western Asia and the multiple interactions between its cities, there came a rapid and widespread revival of the traditions of Hellenistic culture, followed by a general expansion of intellectual curiosity, the transplantation into Arabic literature of the physical and natural sciences, astrology, Hellenistic themes in tales and romances, and a new interest in geographical works and travels in foreign countries.

At the other end of the scale was an urban proletariat of poor artisans, freedmen, and slaves. In between, there grew up a floating population of commission-men, agents, traveling teachers, poets, and vagrants of all kinds. The social and economic grievances of these classes were exploited by the Shīʿite opponents of the orthodox institution, but their successes among the beduins of the Syrian desert, the cultivators in Lower Iraq, and the proletariat of the cities created only nuclei of social disorder, without constructive objects or cultural ideals. Far more important for the development of Islamic culture was the "reformed" Fāṭimid Ismāʿīlī movement towards the end of the third century, which deliberately aimed at building up a new religious institution on the basis of the integration of Islam with Hellenistic culture, and at enlisting the new educated classes in its support. The leaders of the movement set up regular centers for systematic instruction and organized an extensive missionary propaganda. The popular masses were not neglected, and in the city lodges or guilds were constituted for craftsmen.[3] By the date of the transfer of the Fāṭimid Caliphate

[3] The evidence for this is inferential, but fairly convincing; see B. Lewis, "The Islamic Guilds," *Economic History Review,* VIII, 1 (November 1937).

from Tunisia to Cairo (A.D. 973) the whole Muslim world was honeycombed with Fāṭimid agencies.

The significance of the Fāṭimid movement in the Islamic Renaissance is not to be measured only by the contributions of its professed adherents or sympathizers (such as Al-Rāzī and Al-Fārābī in philosophy; 'Alī b. Yūnus in astronomy; Ibn al-Haitham in physics and optics; Māsawaih and 'Alī b. Riḍwān in medicine; the treatises of the Ikhwān al-Ṣafā in the natural sciences), but by the encouragement which it gave to intellectual activities of all kinds, even among its political or religious opponents, and its influence long survived the fall of the Fāṭimid Caliphate in A.D. 1171. It spread a spirit of free enquiry, individual endeavor, and interaction of ideas, which expressed itself in the works of almost all the outstanding writers of Persia and Iraq in the fourth century [A.H.], and most notably in Ibn Sīnā (Avicenna), and found echoes even in Muslim Spain, in spite of the restrictive tendencies of the orthodox Mālikī school and the Almoravid rulers.

For a short time, this advance and diffusion of learning took on something of the character of an organic movement, spreading to every part of the Islamic world, irrespective of political and sectarian boundaries. A new power of intellectual organization was manifested, new methods or combinations were tried out, new types of production evolved in which to present the results of scientific study and literary culture in intelligible form to men of general education, great libraries were built up and observatories founded. The old social divisions between Arab and non-Arab were obliterated in the new civilization and even those which separated Muslims from non-Muslims were softened. Jewish and Christian scholars participated in all intellectual activities on an equality with Muslim scholars; this reflected also upon their social status, and admitted them to an honorable place in the bureaucracy and the public services, though they continued to be exposed from time to time to popular excesses. The leaders of orthodoxy themselves were drawn into the general current to the extent of underpinning its dogmatic foundations by a natural theology derived from prevalent scientific theories; but they were fully conscious of the heretical tendencies present in many branches of study and maintained a jealous independence of the inverse efforts of men like Ibn Sīnā to relate the prevailing philosophical theories to the principles of Islam.

In general, therefore, the consequence of this intellectual expansion was to broaden the whole range of the Arabic humanities by the incorporation of the legacy of Hellenistic culture, which survived as a permanent element in the Arabic-Islamic cultural tradition, uneasily yoked with the religious and old Arabic disciplines. In the arts and architecture also there was a parallel expansion, as the old pre-Muslim arts, Hellenistic, Syrian, and Persian were revived, developed, and diffused, with the requisite adaptations, to create a new Muslim art, whose cultural foundations and significance, however, have not yet been adequately studied.

The Islamic Renaissance suffered, on the other hand, from serious weaknesses. It was a culture and a civilization of the city, which confirmed the already marked urban character of the orthodox culture, arising out of the association of the orthodox institution with government. The immense economic development of the cities completed this process by the concentration of wealth and intellectual activities in them, to the exclusion of the countryside, which had little or no share in the developing civilization, and remained divided from the cities by a widening social gulf. Furthermore, even within the cities, the instability and inorganic character of the political institutions, and the social tensions which prevented the development of municipal institutions, offered a constant threat to cultural activities outside the range of orthodoxy, which itself maintained an ambiguous attitude towards them. Hence, with all the remarkable intellectual achievement of the Islamic Renaissance, its foundations remained shallow, rooted neither in the deep soil of the Islamic movement nor in strong social organisms. It was confined to a narrow (if for the time being widespread and prosperous) layer of urban society, and dependent on temporary factors. So long as a flourishing urban civilization existed, local retractions in one region might be counterbalanced by expansion in another, but its survival was bound up with the survival of the temporary factors to which it owed its existence.

VII

The orthodox revival in the fifth century (the eleventh of the Christian era) [of the Hijra] marks the turning point in the history of Islamic culture. It began as a systematic effort to remove or counteract all the factors of instability and disunity—political, social, religious, and moral—within the Muslim Community, but led ultimately, as will be seen, to a thoroughgoing revolution.

The peculiarly inorganic character of the political institutions during the two preceding centuries was due partly to the conflict with the orthodox institution in the third century [A.H.] and partly to the composition of the military forces. The result of the former had been to delimit sharply the functions of the political institution, confining the activities of the governors to maintenance of order and public security, military policy, and financial administration. All other functions—the administration of law,[4] education, social institutions—remained the jealously guarded preserve of the religious authorities. The religious institution thus interposed between government and subjects, and claimed their exclusive loyalty as the true representatives of Islamic authority. So long, however, as the army was recruited from among the subjects directly, or though the association of the feudal nobles with the government, there still remained a positive link between rulers and people. When this was removed by the formation of professional armies of slaves and mercenaries no organic relation was left; the only remaining connection was the tax-gathering function. It has been well said that in medieval Islam there were never real "states" but only "empires" more or less extensive, and that the only political unity was the ideological but powerful concept of the *Dār al-Islām,* the common homeland of all Muslims.[5]

The indifference, passing into hostility, of the general population to the political organizations made the existence and survival of rulers, dynasties and regimes dependent, with rare exceptions, on the

[4] Except for special administrative courts for the army and bureaucracy.

[5] J. H. Kramers, *Proceedings of the XXII International Congress of Orientalists,* Istanbul, 1953, p. 94. See also the article "Dār al-Islām" in *Encyclopedia of Islam,* Leyden and London, 1913-34.

quality of their military forces. Since the religious institution was, for the reasons already given, precluded from acting effectively as a mediating force, the political history of the later third and fourth centuries [A.H.] was mainly occupied by the struggle between Caliphs, princes, and armed forces for power eventually won, in every case, by the army commanders. Thus the fourth century saw the complete breakdown of the political organization built up by the Caliph on the Roman and Persian foundations. The final blow was given during the century of Shī'ite governments in Western Asia, an era of widespread misrule and anarchy, which bore most heavily on the countryside, although the disorders and ideological divisions affected the cities also in varying degrees.

The urban communities in all parts of the medieval Muslim world have one remarkable feature in common: the development of more or less organized popular parties, and the frequency of violent outbreaks either between them or against the government. This may be explained partly by the nomadic heritage of many citizens, partly by the existence of a large proletariat, whose grievances were championed or exploited by local reformers or agitators, often in combination with anti-Sunnī movements. Examples may be found in the standing feud in Baghdad between the Sunnīs and the Shī'ites, and the anti-Ismā'īlī riots of the Karrāmites in the Persian cities. But as often the rival parties were of the same sect, or of different orthodox schools, as in the feuds between Ḥanafites and Shāfi'ites in Khūrasān. Lawlessness on the part of the troops led repeatedly to the formation of citizen organizations for defence and reprisals, which sometimes became no more than robber gangs. This lack of internal unity in the cities, sharpened by the mutual suspicions of proletariat, merchants and governors, even found physical expression in their organization in separate and independent quarters, with their own defenses. In such features, as well as in the absence of leadership by the merchant classes (who were inclined to keep out of public life), are probably to be found the reasons for the failure of the medieval Islamic cities to develop organized municipal institutions.

The orthodox revival began at the end of the fourth century [A.H.] in Khūrasān, the one important region in Western Asia which had not fallen under Shī'ite government, apparently in response to the challenge of the organized missionary activities of the Fāṭimids on the one hand, and the consolidation of "Twelver" Shī'ism into a rival religious institution during the century of Shī'ite rule in Western Persia and Iraq. Early in the fifth century [A.H.], the Shāfi'ites were organizing orthodox colleges (known as *madrasas*) in imitation of the Fāṭimid missionary institutions. But the revival had also a political aim: the liberation of the Caliphate from Shī'ite control. In pursuance of their object, the Sunnī leaders formed what amounted to an alliance with the Seljuk leaders of the immigrating Turkish tribes from the East, an alliance formally ratified by the Caliph himself after the Seljuk conquest of Western Persia and Iraq (A.D. 1055).

The renewed association under the Seljuks of the ruling and orthodox institutions was drawn still closer by the initiative of the vizier Nizām al-Mulk in founding Nizāmīya *madrasas*. These were not only religious seminaries for directing and systematizing higher education, but training colleges in the Arabic humanities for a new class of administrators, the "orthodox bureaucracy" which replaced the former secretarial class, and in the Seljuk empire and its successors held a place as directors of civil administration alongside the military governors of provinces and cities. Yet at the same time the functional division between the ruling and religious institutions was more sharply defined than ever by the formal constitution of the Sultanate, as the organ of political and military administration, alongside (though ideally subordinate to) the Caliphate, as the head of the religious institution. It was the same Nizām al-Mulk who reaffirmed this duality by restating his *Siyāsat-nāma,*[6] the old Persian tradition of monarchy, with its independent ethical standards based on force and opportunism, thus perpetuating the inner disharmony which has always proved to be the principal weakness of Islam as a politico-social organism.

Nevertheless, by the device of forming an administrative class belonging to the religious institution and setting it alongside the secular governors, it is probable that something more was aimed at than a merely formal link between them. It is reasonably certain that one object was to preserve the spiritual independence of the

[6] Edited and translated by Ch. Schefer, Paris, 1891-93.

orthodox institution against the increasing power and absolutism of the temporal princes, and at the same time to maintain (or to re-create) the unity of the Community. Each party was expected to find its own interest in supporting the other; "kingship and religion are twins." A further measure of Nizām al-Mulk indicates his strong sense of social order. Both the military organization and the bureaucratic institution were assimilated to the old (and by now almost extinct) Persian landowning class by a reconstructed feudal system. Thus by the dual means of association with the religious institution and tying the army to the soil, the ruling institution would regain in some measure the organic character which it had lost. By the same association the religious institution would gain the support of the ruling institution in its efforts to re-create unity; for it must not be forgotten that the orthodox revival was a deliberate reaction against the experience of division during the period of Shī'ite governments.

The same pursuit of unity is manifest in the gradual concentration of all higher education, both for religious and public service, in the new *madrasas*. It is improbable that this was deliberately designed to narrow down education and circumscribe intellectual activities, by control and patronage, to the religious and philological sciences. The fact of narrowing down was rather the natural consequence of this concentration combined with other factors. First, it was inevitable that the attempt should be made to bring all other studies into an organic relation with the religious and literary interests of the *madrasa*; this involved some degree of standardization, and the teaching of these standardized materials in the authoritarian manner already described. Second, once the Hellenistic elements were assimilated into the Arabic humanities there were no new elements from outside which could be brought into Islamic culture to challenge the established disciplines or give a fresh impulse to intellectual development.[7] Third, the inner decline of urban culture (to be described later) brought with it a narrowing down of intellectual interests.

For some centuries however, the influences of the Islamic Renais-

[7] The only exception to this was the Chinese influence mediated at a later date through the Mongols, but this was fleeting and peripheral, and left an effective mark only in the domain of art in the further Eastern provinces.

sance remained active within the orthodox institution, and were not entirely crushed out by the process of standardization. Intellectual energies found new outlets in place of philosophical, scientific, and secular studies. It is instructive to observe the consequences of the Sunnī revival movement in Syria and Egypt under Nuraddin and Saladin and their successors (under whom a powerful orthodox bureaucracy maintained an exceptionally close association with the rulers). After the general decay of cultural life in the later Fāṭimid period, the introduction of the organized Niẓāmīya type of education brought an outburst of intellectual life, literature and cultural activities of many kinds, including a revival of art and architecture. For two centuries they remained at a high level before beginning to be affected by the germs of decay from standardization and the increasing subordination of the orthodox institution to the Mamlūk military aristocracy.

At the same time, the Sunnī revival aimed at eradicating Shī'ism not only as a political force, but as an element of moral disunity. This proved to be, on the whole, surprisingly easy. In the intellectual field Shi'ite dogmatics were smothered by the formulation of orthodox dogmatics in final and authoritative treatises. Among the general public the earlier sympathetic attitude towards Shī'ism was largely dissipated by the century of Shī'ite misgovernment and the weakness of the later Fāṭimids. But the orthodox leaders wisely gave satisfaction to the emotional attachment felt for the house of 'Alī by incorporating the Shī'ite shrines as objects of veneration within the orthodox Community. Shī'ism survived only in fragmentary groups, particularly among the tribesmen of Lower Iraq; and the activist movement of neo-Ismā'īlīs or "Assassins," organized in the mountainous fringes of Northern Persia and Northern Syria, gained no following in spite of its terrorist campaign against the orthodox rulers and bureaucracy, but rather strengthened the movement of Sunnī reunion by the hostility which it aroused.

The Sunnī revival, linked with Seljuk expansion, achieved by these means a striking success in reuniting and integrating at a common level the whole urban culture of Western Asia and Egypt. The rapidity of the process, however, and the solidity of the results indicate that it did not so much create this unity as bring to fruition already existing trends. The foundations had in fact been laid during the preceding centuries by the slow but persistent pressure of the standardized Sharī'ah law in remoulding the social ethics and institutions of all Muslims, and substituting its common processes and attitudes for their divergent older traditions. There still remained, however, the problem of the social divisions and antagonisms within the cities, and, related to it, the problem of extending the influence of the orthodox religious movement to the populations outside urban radius.

VIII

Among the established agricultural populations within the Islamic lands, it is generally possible to trace the gradual advance of the influence of the Sharī'ah. But from the fifth century [A.H.] conditions were radically changed in all parts of the Muslim world by the resurgence of the nomads: the irruption of Turkish tribes in East and North Persia, Mesopotamia and North Syria; Arab tribal movements in Syria, Egypt, and North Africa; Berber movements in North Africa. In large areas the substitution of pastoral for agricultural economy led to economic retrogression; and although the nomads were kept in relative check at first by Seljuk imperial power, from the middle of the sixth century [A.H.] they were throwing off all control, and reducing the cities in Persia and the northern provinces to islands of "oasis culture," dependent for their survival on armed garrisons of imperial troops or the forces of local princes. Thus at the very moment when the orthodox institution had succeeded in integrating the urban culture of Islam under its aegis, that culture itself was increasingly hemmed in by the nomadic expansion and endangered by the immigration of new Turkish tribes who were not even nominally Muslim.

In these circumstances, the leaders of the orthodox institution began to realize the value of the revivalist missions led by Sūfī preachers among the urban proletariat and in the countryside, which they had hitherto regarded with some suspicion and hostility. The pietist missionaries who labored to produce conversions among the artisans and proletariat were inclined to share the proletariat's suspicions of the orthodox institution, as too closely identified with the political powers, even if they were still more strongly opposed to sectarian divisions and activist movements of all kinds. They disliked, moreover, the intellectualizing tendencies in orthodox theology, which seemed to emphasize external profession to the detriment of personal devotion. The orthodox leaders, for their part, distrusted the mystical and gnostic currents which were flowing into Sufism from the older Asian religions, the theosophical claims to union with the Divine, and the organized religious exercises for its adherents which threatened to displace the mosque rituals.

But the spiritual vitality of the Sūfī movement could not be denied, and indeed some accommodation with it was forced upon the orthodox leaders by imperative circumstances. Long before the Seljuk invasion, Sūfī missionaries had extended their activities into and beyond the frontier areas, and had been instrumental in the conversion of the Turkish tribes, among whom consequently, their influence was greater than that of the orthodox doctors. The association of the Sunnī reaction with the Seljuks thus reopened the question of the relations between the Sūfīs and the orthodox institution. It was not an easy problem for the theologians, however, in their quest for unity, to integrate the Sūfī movement in the orthodox religious institution, until the great theologian Al-Ghazālī (d. 505/1111), in his most important work,[8] demonstrated the truly Islamic foundation of Sufism, and reconciled both by the argument that orthodoxy without the revivalist leaven of Sufism was an empty profession, and Sufism without orthodoxy dangerous subjectivism.

Henceforward, in the movement of reunion the religious institution is represented both by the orthodox institution (including the religious bureaucracy) and by the Sūfī shaikhs, with the special function of missionary work in the cities and countryside. Everywhere Sūfī convents were founded simultaneously with *madrasas,* and on the whole the leaders of both wings cooperated with relatively little friction or jealousy. Gradually however, the Sūfī movement, organizing itself as a rival institution, drained the orthodox institution of most of its vigor and vitality, and finally, when the dwindling of the religious bureaucracy in face of the encroachments

[8] Entitled *Iḥyā' 'ulūm al-dīn,* "The Revival of the Religious Sciences." In his earlier works Al-Ghazālī had summed up and consolidated the intellectual foundations of the orthodox revival in relation to dogmatics, the Hellenistic sciences, and the argument against the Shi'ites. See A. J. Wensinck, *La Penseé de Ghazzali,* Paris, 1940.

of the ruling military classes in Egypt and India reduced the orthodox institution to a dangerous dependence on the ruling institution, finally found itself the champion of spiritual independence against both the rulers and the official 'ulamā'.

From the seventh [to the] thirteenth centuries, moreover, Sufism increasingly attracted the creative social and intellectual energies within the Community, to become the bearer or instrument of a social and cultural revolution—a process hastened on by the destruction of the still vigorous centers of Islamic culture in North Persia during the Mongol invasion of 1220 [A.D.] and the Mongol occupation of all Western Asia (except Syria) after the capture of Baghdad in 1258. The orthodox institution was eclipsed under the rule of the heathen princes, and though it gradually revived in the following century its social and political foundations were too weak to allow it to recover its former influence. Its function of maintaining the unity of the Community thus passed to the Sūfī movement in new and difficult circumstances. This fact itself determined that the Sūfī methods of operation would differ from those of the orthodox institution, but was also in keeping with their own historical origins. In contrast to the orthodox institution, the Sūfī movement was based on popular appeal, and its new structure of religious unity was built on popular foundations. It would be difficult to prove (or even to imagine) that the Sūfī leaders consciously formulated a plan of action, and the result was achieved in a manner which gives the impression of spontaneous action initiated independently and almost simultaneously in both eastern and western lands of Islam.

This development arose out of two cardinal elements in Sufism: the close personal relation between the Sūfī shaikh and his disciples, and its missionary spirit. Whereas in the early centuries, the Sūfī circles were individual and dispersed units, the loose proliferation of individual activities was now replaced by more organized structures. Regular colleges were founded, with the aid of benefactions and alms, by particular shaikhs, who commissioned their leading disciples, after training in the special rites and rules of the "order," to organize daughter colleges in other centers and regions, and these maintained a close association with the original college and the successors of its founder.

Such networks of affiliated colleges and convents constituted a "path" (*ṭarīqa*). Their function was not only to train initiates but to serve as centers of religious instruction and spiritual influence among the general population, who were associated with the order as "lay members." At some stage, not yet definitely established, lay membership was integrated with the guild organizations of artisans and other professions, each guild or corporation being affiliated to a particular *ṭarīqa,* and extended also to village and tribal areas. While many *ṭarīqas* had only local importance, the greater orders (such as the Qādirī, Shādhilī, and Suhrawardī) spread over the whole or a large part of Islamic territory. Thus they contributed, even more effectively than the orthodox institution (but at the same time building upon the foundations laid in earlier centuries by the common authority of the *Sharī'ah*), to maintain the ideal unity of all Muslims, in spite of a very few Shī'ite *ṭarīqas* and of deviation from strict orthodoxy among the initiates of some more extreme orders.

It was not only the physical expansion of the great *ṭarīqas,* however, that served the cause of unity. Teachers and disciples journeyed from end to end of the Muslim world, bearing the seeds of interchange and cross-fertilization within the Sūfī framework. While this had been a characteristic of Islamic culture from the early centuries, its importance was now immensely increased. One consequence of the Turkish immigrations and Mongol invasions was to harden the division of the Muslim lands into separate Arabic, Persian, and Turkish linguistic regions, between which literary intercommunication was confined to restricted circles of the educated. Although the effects of this division can be seen also in the distribution of the *ṭarīqas,* the activities of the Sūfī teachers did much to counteract them by furnishing a means for the transference of ideas across linguistic frontiers and guiding their further development on parallel lines.

How effective the communication of ideas was between the initiates in every region is strikingly shown by a development which was to prove of decisive significance for the future cultural action and influence of Sufism—the evolution of its own intellectual system and literature. In its pure essence, Sufism, being a personal religious attitude emphasizing intuitive experience against rational knowledge, could insofar as it added to or diverged from the Sharī'ah basis of Islam, present no common body of doctrine. But it was inevitable that as institutional forms developed with organized teaching certain doctrinal tendencies should crystallize within them. The general trend was towards pantheism; but in the major orders these tendencies were stabilized in one or other of two related philosophies. One was illuminationist, deriving ultimately from Asiatic gnosticism and systematized by Yaḥyā al-Suhrawardī;[9] the other was monist, deriving from popular Hellenistic philosophy (probably through the Fāṭimid literature), and expounded by the Spanish Arab Muḥyi'l-dīn Ibn al-'Arabī.[10] The former was widely disseminated in the eastern provinces; the latter at first in the Arabic and Turkish orders, but later also in the East.

The intellectual consequences of this were extremely grave. Instead of revitalizing the inert matter of scholastic instruction in the *madrasas,* it drew intellectual energies off into subjective and antirational speculation, leaving the former more inert than ever and supplying no rigorous intellectual discipline in its place. On the other hand—emphasizing the social function of Sufism as an expression of cultural unity—these mystical institutions and adumbrations were enshrined in a new poetical literature, which utilized popular literary forms (wine-songs, love-songs, romances, apologues) and transposed or transformed their imagery into religious symbolism. These productions, spread over all the Muslim world, in Arabic, Persian, or Turkish, were appreciated by all classes and for several centuries all but monopolized literary and aesthetic creation. The greater part of prose literature followed in their wake, furnishing in its higher ranges commentaries (in the true scholastic tradition) on the works of the masters and their successors or on the great Persian poems, and in its lower ranges lives and legends of saints and other devotional works.

Finally the Sūfī movement, in spite of its original quietism and pacifism, took too firm root in the social organization of the Muslim peoples not to have also political effects. Especially in regions, such as Persia and Anatolia after the collapse of Mongol rule, where cen-

[9] Executed for heresy at Aleppo in 1191. See *Shihāb-al-Dīn Yaḥyā al-Suhrawardī: Opera Metaphysica et Mystica,* ed. H. Corbin, vol. I, Istanbul, 1945, Introduction.

[10] Died at Damascus 1240. See A. E. Affifi, *The Mystical Philosophy of Muhyid dīn-Ibnul 'Arabī,* Cambridge, 1939.

tralized political institutions had broken down by dynastic disruption of nomadization, the Sūfī brotherhood was often the only form of social organization left. It naturally served, in consequence, as the basis of association for self-defense against the violence of local tyrants or tribesmen, and in favorable conditions developed into a fighting force, emulating the achievements of the primitive Muslim armies "in the path of God." The inner history of Northern Persia in the fourteenth and fifteenth [A.D.] centuries is obscure, but it seems probable that most political movements had Sūfī affiliations of some kind. In contemporary Anatolia, the town artisans were organized in *akhī* guilds, the tribal revolts led by Sūfī shaikhs, and most of the small principalities were "*ghāzi* states," devoted to war against the infidel and organized in corporations led by amīrs but frequently, if not in all cases, associated with a Sūfī *ṭarīqa*. Of the two great empires which were to divide Western Asia between them until the twentieth century, it has been shown fairly conclusively that the Ottoman Empire began as such a "*ghāzi* state," [11] and there is no question that its rival, the Safavid kingdom of Persia, was created by the shaikhs of the Safavī suborder of the Suhrawardī *ṭarīqa*.[12]

Thus through the influence and activity of Sufism the Islamic world was entirely transformed from the thirteenth century [A.D.] onwards—spiritually, morally, intellectually, imaginatively, and even politically—and only the orthodox *madrasas* preserved a tenuous link with the cultural tradition of medieval Islam.

[11] See on this, and on conditions on Anatolia generally. P. Wittek, *The Rise of the Ottoman Empire*, London, 1938, especially pp. 33-40.

[12] See W. Hinz, *Irans Aufstieg zum Nationalstaat im fünfzehnten Jahrhundert*, Berlin-Leipzig, 1936.

2

ISLAM IN A HUMANISTIC EDUCATION

◆◄◉►◆

G. E. von Grunebaum

A humanistic education guides the individual through self-cognition to right action. Self-cognition is contingent on a realization of the individual's position in the world, metaphysical and social, and an understanding of what made him and the world what they are. Action will not be right unless it relates meaningfully the personality of the agent and the requirements of his society.

A humanistic education will essay to evoke the widest possible range of responses to the stimuli of civilization. It will expose the individual to respresentative specimens of the several fields of cultural endeavor and a large selection of significant facts designed to supplement, and to enrich the context of, personal experience. The individual data are centered on a concept of the nature of man from which is derived the knowledge of how he must act to preserve his dignity as a person and a member of society and to widen the collectively conquered area of civilization.

A humanistic education is a guided process of progressive self-interpretation, aspiring after a principle or principles through which the totality of human experience can be organized and understood in essence and development. The closer the human reality is apprehended, the closer will right action be approximated.

To a humanistic education as administered within the civilization

Reprinted from *The Journal of General Education,* IV (1949) 12-31, by permission of the University of Chicago Press. Copyright © 1949 by the University of Chicago. Some of the footnotes have been omitted.

of the West the consideration of Islam commends itself on these grounds:

1. Islam presents the spectacle of the development of a world religion in the full light of history.

2. It presents the further spectacle of the widening of this religion into a civilization.

3. In the development of this Islamic civilization foreign cultural traditions were absorbed, modified, and again eliminated. Some of these traditions have also gone into the making of the West. Thus the growth and decline of Islamic civilization between the seventh and the twelfth centuries A.D. illuminate almost dramatically the processes of cultural interaction and culture transformation, as well as the concept of cultural influence as such.

4. Islamic civilization constitutes a complete system of thought and behavior growing out of a fundamental impulse and enveloping man in all his relations: to God, the universe, and himself. This system is both close enough to the Western view of the world to be intellectually and emotionally understandable and sufficiently far removed from it to deepen, by contrast, the self-interpretation of the West.

I

Like Christianity and Manichaeanism, Islam is a revealed religion in which the person of the revealing agent forms an integral part of the faith. It is not sufficient to believe in the message brought the Arabs by Muḥammad, the son of 'Abdallâh, of Mecca (ca. A.D. 570–June 8, 632); it is also imperative to believe in the significance of the election, by the Lord, of Muḥammad and none other as the Seal of the Prophets. The creed links the two fundamental verities: "I testify that there is no god but God (Allâh) and that Muḥammad is the Messenger of God."

To himself, Muḥammad is a mere man; there is no claim to consubstantiality, in whatever guise, with the divinity; he is no thaumaturge, although he is frequently pressured to perform miracles in substantiation of his mission. His one and only miracle is the Book, as it has been in one form or another the evidentiary and intellectual center of any respectable faith since the last centuries B.C.; and this miracle is his, only insofar as it is given to and through him. Whenever he is not guided by direct revelation, he is fallible in thought and deed. He does not consider himself the exemplar on which the faithful are to model their lives, although, as time went by, his came to be considered the ideal life and his personality the quintessence of perfection, human and superhuman; and, in yielding to the changing dreams of the ages, he was understood as the great ascetic, the intercessor with God for the believers, the mystic saint, the miracleworker with knowledge of the hidden, the descendant of Adam and heir of his spark of divine substance, the cause of creation, the hub of the universe.

God's message is universal but is conveyed to different peoples by different messengers and at different times. Each messenger is sent to his own people with a partial version in his own tongue of the Book's heavenly prototype. There have been many such messengers in the past—tradition knows of 124,000—but with Muḥammad, who was vouchsafed the final and most perfect message, the end of Revelation has been reached. It is the very identity of his message with that of his predecessors like Moses and Jesus that vouches for Muḥammad's veracity. When, to his profound dismay, the Jews and Christians failed to recognize their scriptures in his teachings, Muḥammad realized that they had falsified their original Revelation and that God had sent him to restore the unadulterated religion of Abraham, the father of Ishmael, the ancestor of the Arabs. Before Muḥammad, Marcion and Mani had already developed the notion that the disciples inevitably corrupt the doctrine of the master; and Mani, at least, had taken great care to prevent this fate from happening to his ideas. Muḥammad was successful to the extent that the text of his Book has come down to us undistorted.

It would seem that Arab paganism, never systemized or given a philosophic skeleton, had been losing its grip during the sixth century A.D. It had been a faith of great local variations, with astral coloring among the more civilized groups, but everywhere still close to primitive fetishistic forms of worship. Mecca, a commercial community that had grown up around the sanctuary of the Ka'ba and a cosmopolitan town, harbored a sizable foreign population, many of them Jews and Christians of a sort; and there is evidence of a feeling of religious dissatisfaction and of a seeking for something new, something purer and intellectually more substantial than the inherited and but lukewarmly held polytheism. The age had begun to be concerned with the Hereafter. It was the fear of the End, the trembling before the Judgment to which Muḥammad gave expression in his first inspired utterances. By turning away from the idols that are but wood or stone and accepting the truth of the one and only God, the Creator and Lord of heaven and earth, man could win rescue from the horrors of the Day and the eternal punishment that was to be meted out soon; for it was rescue rather than salvation that the age craved and that Muḥammad offered. People found themselves frightened and conscious of their evil deeds. The Fire was threatening them, and they yearned for protection. But they did not feel sinful to the core, corrupt in their essence, laboring under the metaphysical consequences of a Fall. No original sin had to be expunged. They were not in need of salvation through divine self-sacrifice, they needed information as to the true God and as to the behavior that he demanded. Islam has never developed sacramental mysteries, it has remained faithful to the impulse of its origin by showing erring man the path to paradise in a purely rational, almost technical, manner. But man, rewarded or punished, remains man—God does not descend to earth to lift man beyond himself. In fact, as apologetic and polemic literature amply testifies, to this very day the concept of the suffering God as well as the complementary concepts of original sin and salvation from sin have remained alien to Islam to the point of being intellectually incomprehensible, owing to the utter foreignness of the *Lebensgefühl* that evoked the longings and the doctrines to satisfy them.

The immediate means of attaining this rescue and of meeting this emergency of the impending catastrophe was the acceptance of monotheism under the guidance of the Lord's authorized Messenger. It is not easy to gauge when Muḥammad abandoned his terrifying vision of the End of the World as close by; but, as time wore on, his anxiety was somewhat calmed by a realization of the indefinite postponement of the hour. What . . . took the early Christians decades to accept, Muḥammad acknowledged after a very few years—as the Lord was pleased to continue this world for a further reprieve, short or long, his community had to be settled in it in complete conformance with his revealed instructions. So it became the task of the community to evolve a comprehensive pattern for a life under God, covering every phase of human existence from conception to burial and eliminating any distinction between the sacred and the profane aspects of life by making every instant of it religiously relevant and requiring ritualistic perfection for the performance of any action whatsoever. In this manner behavior was stereotyped to a point, but the whole of life, down to its most repulsive detail, was given the supreme dignity of religious significance. And not only the life of the individual to be transformed into a sequence of divinely required acts, but Muslim society as a whole was to be equally transformed: the state, the army, the treasury became in the terminology of the early believers the state of God, the army of God, the treasury of God.

It is the quest for the correct life that stands out as the supreme motive of the Islamic experiment; it is the conflict between this life and the exigencies of this world (frequently personified to the pious as lawless rulers, hypocrites, and heretics) that largely dominates the internal history of Islam. The increasingly narrow and worried interpretation of the ideal that had early become, in its elaboration and administration, the vested interest of a class of jurist-theologians would seem to bear most of the guilt of the corroding discord between fiction and reality that, in the later Middle Ages, pervades Muslim society more profoundly than it does, of necessity, any human organization.

The relatively minor role of doctrine as contrasted with behavior is reflected in the five "pillars" of Islam, the fundamental obligations imposed on each and every believer. The Prophet is supposed to have said: "Islam is built upon five things, testimony that there is no god but God and that Muḥammad is the Messenger of God; prayer; the poor-rate; pilgrimage [to Mecca]; and fast in Ramaḍân." [1]

Correctness as the basic purpose of life makes for authoritarianism. Duties and doctrine can be accepted as binding only when imposed by, or derived from, a source that is beyond human questioning. Directly or indirectly any regulation should go back to the Lord himself. The Koran (*Qur'ân,* from Syriac *qeryânâ, lectio,* and lec-

[1] Quoted by D. B. Macdonald, *Development of Muslim Theology, Jurisprudence, and Constitutional Theory* (New York, 1903), p. 292.

tionary) as the collection of all preserved revelations—undertaken under the caliph 'Uthmân (644-56)—in other words, the direct speech of the Lord addressed to Muḥammad, is marked out as the foremost authority. To the Muslim, the Koran treats of every subject, but more specifically of matters of faith, legal prescriptions, and prophetic history. The first Arabic book, composed in frequently relaxed prose and put together from records of the individual revelations in a somewhat arbitrary manner, the Koran contains, especially in its eschatological *sûras* or sections, many a beautiful passage. In mastering the difficulties of expressing trains of thought not hitherto articulated in Arabic, Muḥammad shows himself a literary innovator of considerable stature. A certain clumsiness, say, in legal formulations[2] is as palpable as is the defective technique of narration when it comes to telling complex stories of former prophets and the like, particularly when the koranic style is compared with the matchless grace and precision with which Arabic authors present narrative material. To the Muslim, however, the Koran as the Word of God is inimitable in point of diction, and the desire to explain its stylistic uniqueness has been one powerful impulse toward the development of an Arabic theory of literature. Muslims are agreed that the Koran requires philological explanation; they are not agreed on the extent to which exegesis is admissible. But as faith necessitates the harmonization of the personal or the school viewpoint with Revelation, philosophical, mystical, and any kind of partisan exegesis, best served by allegorical interpretation, is unavoidable.

But, even upon acceptance of a generous measure of interpretative elasticity, the Koran will not resolve every problem of the religious life. It is necessary to fall back on the *sunna,* the prophetic custom or tradition, as a second authority. In the absence of a koranic line, a private saying of the Prophet or a contemporary report on his behavior in a given situation will be decisive. The more in the consciousness of the community the Messenger was transformed into a thaumaturge, the more easily could political prophesies *ex eventu,* school doctrines, and, in general, sayings reflecting the state of mind

[2] Cf., e.g., Koran 2:282-83, on recording of debts. The best and most recent English translation of the Koran by R. Bell (Edinburgh, 1937-39) offers an analysis of the 114 *sûras* or chapters.

of the times be ascribed to him. To the community, the *sunna* acquired an importance that allowed it to override on occasion the express statement of the Book itself. This willingness to accept reality under a relatively thin disguise of prophetic indorsement is more clearly evident in the recognition of the consensus of the community as a third authority after Koran and *sunna*. Methodologically justified by the alleged words of Muḥammad, "My community will never be agreed on an error," the *ijmâ'* of the learned that does not make decisions of a programmatic character but only states what has become common (and therewith binding) practice and belief has permitted the integration into Islam of essentially "anti-Islamic" elements, such as the cult of saints, and thereby prevented too dangerous a chasm between the traditional norm and the practice of the day.

Nevertheless, Islam has always been traditionalist. The examples to be followed belong to the ever more remote past. Muḥammad's early followers were the best generation; their successors, the second best. From then on, the world has been deteriorating and will continue to deteriorate until it comes to its appointed end. The living generation is not permitted to change the inherited ways—for change must needs be for the worse. Innovation in religious matters (and religion covers everything relevant to the good life) is to be rejected, the innovator liable to punishment. The reformer therefore either adduces prophetic or koranic witness for his proposal or advocates the return to the golden age of primitive Islam. The pattern may not be abandoned or even modified; it may only be stripped of accretions and freed of distortions that have accumulated in the course of time. The heroic, the creative, age is past. . . . The critics fight hard, if unsuccessfully, to contain poetry within the limits of the pre-Islamic tradition and prevent it from adapting to changed conditions and changed emotions. Only in the ninth and tenth centuries is there a feeling of youthfulness in the intellectual world, a feeling that the ancients can be equaled and surpassed. Fatimid propaganda in Africa stresses the youth of the dynasty as opposed to the decrepit regime of the Abbasid house in Baghdad. But this self-confidence is far from being shared by all, and it wanes in the eleventh century without having affected the general attitude of looking backward for the guiding ideals.

The authority of tradition is best upheld by a formalistic approach which gives promise of eliminating the wilfulness of personal reasoning. When the community found itself flooded with an immense and steadily growing number of forged sayings of Muḥammad, criteria for sifting the genuine from the spurious had to be found. Instead of concentrating on an analysis of the content, the collectors studied the chain of witnesses that linked the latest reporter of the apothegm to the Prophet himself. These inquiries laid the ground for impressive biographical studies that remained unparalleled in the West until comparatively recent times, but they failed to provide an obstacle to the learned forger nor did they, to the modern mind, establish the material trustworthiness of the sayings.

Prayer as included among the five "pillars" is ritual prayer, not personal involvement or communion with God. It consists of a fairly complicated sequence of formulas that are recited in coordination with a sequence of exactly prescribed body-movements. Ablution and the covering of (parts of) the body are two necessary preliminaries. The prayers are to be performed five times a day at stated times, preferably in common, in the mosque, and behind a prayer-leader. Immense attention has been given by the canon lawyers to the detail of the performance and to any accidental circumstance that might invalidate it. Ghazzâlî (d. 1111), perhaps the greatest theologian of Islam, has to combat their view that it is the outward acts and utterances rather than the inner attitude that determines the validity of the prayer. He defines the limitations of the law:

> [Canon lawyers] build up the external side of the laws of the religion upon the external side of the acts of the members, since the external side of the acts is a sufficient guard against being killed or chastised by the sultan. As to whether the external side of these acts benefits in the next abode, this is not within the bounds of canon law, because it is not possible to claim agreement on this point.[3]

Islam is permeated by a sense of the Autocracy of the Lord. The Lord is One, All-Powerful, not bound by the moral law, in no way obliged to give man right guidance or to reward and punish him according to his obedience or disobedience. The greatness of Allâh

[3] *Iḥyâ' 'ulûm ad-dîn* (Bulâq, 1289/1872), I, 156, trans. E. E. Calverly, *Worship in Islam* (Madras, India, 1925), p. 90.

is emphasized through the helpless weakness of man, his most illustrious creature. It seems rather obvious that the real reason for the Muslim denial of laws of nature, of an eternal order of things by which God binds himself to abide, is due not so much to dialectical considerations as to the overpowering impulse to revel in the contemplation of Allâh's unrestrained majesty, even though it is at the cost of man's self-abasement and the injection of an element of whimsicality in the government of the universe. The apparent causal regularity of events reflects not irrevocable law but the Lord's habitual procedure. Like the benevolent despot on earth whose absurdly magnified reflection he is, the Lord is, on the whole, kindly inclined toward his creatures and disposed to lighten the burden of their obligations, to take a lenient view of their efforts, and to be approachable by his favorites—especially the Prophet Muḥammad—when they intercede for the erring believer. Orthodox Islam is imbued with the realization, shared by (if not inherited from) the Gnostic world and later on by Calvin and Pascal, that an act of awakening, transforming grace will always have to precede man's own effort to draw near God. With merciless precision the Koran declares: "We have created for Gehenna (Hell) many of the jinn and of mankind" (Koran 7:178). And again: "Whomsoever He willeth, Allâh sendeth astray, and whomsoever He willeth He setteth on a straight path." [4]

The Mu'tazila, the founders of speculative dogmatics in Islam—the school arises in the eighth century—fought the anthropomorphism of the orthodox concept of God and argued for the strictest possible interpretation of Allâh's unity. But, in teaching that God will always do what is best and wisest for his creation, they limit his arbitrary omnipotence. By coordinating human behavior and the divine reaction on a more conventional moral level, they are clearly animated by a different outlook on man, whose dignity they are asserting and protecting by their emphasis on the Lord's justice. Orthodoxy has never ceased to represent the opposite attitude.

Personal piety in the first generations of believers remained dominated by fear. The greatest religious genius of the period, Ḥasan al-Baṣrî (d. 728), was first and foremost an ascetic of harsh austerity.

[4] Koran 6:39; repeated several times, e.g., 13:27 and 14:4; the translation is that of R. Bell, *The Qur'ân* (Edinburgh, 1937-39).

"The main theme of his teaching and preaching was a call to repentance because of the wrath that was to come, and he urged his hearers to despise this transitory life and all that belonged to this world which perishes. . . . We are told that when Ḥasan heard of a man who would be saved in the end, after a thousand years in Hell, he fell to weeping and said; 'Would that I might be like that man.' "[5] The formalism of man's relations to God as laid down in the canon law and what appeared to many the transformation of religion into jurisprudence directed pious sentiment toward the seeking of an immediate contact with the Lord. Fear and reverence were to be balanced by love and trust. By complete and exclusive devotion, the believer could enter into his Lord's familiarity, be vouchsafed the divine vision, and submerge his own self in ecstasy in the divine essence. Mystic experience bridged the abyss, considered impassable by the theologian, between man and God, leading in some instances to full pantheistic self-identification with the Master. Most rationalizing effort of the mystics was concerned with showing the compatibility of their experience with the orthodox norm, the possibility of reconciling the exclusiveness of the prophetic mission with the personal contact between the mystic adept and his God. Before the latent opposition between the mystic and the official approach had come to a head—in fact, before the theological implications of their mystic approach had completely dawned on its professors—the great woman-saint, Râbi'a al-'Adawiyya (d. ca. 801), spoke to God in inspired unconcern:

I have loved Thee with two loves, a selfish love and a love that is worthy (of Thee),
As for the love which is selfish, I occupy myself therein with remembrance of Thee to the exclusion of all others,
As for that which is worthy of Thee, therein Thou raisest the veil that I may see Thee.
O my Hope and my Rest and my Delight,
The heart can love none other but Thee."[6]

[5] Margaret Smith, *Studies in Early Mysticism in the Near and Middle East* (London, 1931) p. 175.
[6] Margaret Smith, *Râbi'a the Mystic and her Fellow-Saints in Islam* (Cambridge, 1928), pp. 102-3.

Abû Naṣr as-Sarrâj (d. 988) explains that the Sûfîs (literally "those clad in wool," [from] ṣûf)

> agree with the Traditionists and Jurists in their beliefs and accept their sciences and consult them in difficult matters of religious law. Should there be a difference of opinion, the Ṣûfîs always adopt the principle of following the strictest and most perfect course; they venerate the commandments of God and do not seek to evade them. Such is their practice in regard to the formal sciences handled by the Traditionists and Jurists, but having left these behind they rise to heights of mystical devotion and ethical self-culture which are exclusively their own.[7]

The Jurists discuss the Koran and Tradition, but only the Sûfîs realize the feelings referred to by terms such as "repentance," "patience," "fear," and "hope." All Ṣûfism is to be found in the Koran and in the *sunna,* but only the Ṣûfîs have experiental access to these aspects of Revelation. Even had not many a mystic drawn the logical conclusion of his position and deprecated the externals of religion and the keeping of the canonical obligations, the contradictory aspirations pursued by the jurists and the mystics would have carried the threat of the disintegration of the very basis of Islam. To the jurist-theologian the mystic's indifference to doctrine appeared both impious and antisocial, while to the mystic the rationalization of the ineffable with its scholastic niceties seemed insignificant. Jalâl ad-Dîn Rûmî (d. 1273) said:

> This doctrine has become the adversary and bitter enemy of that, so that the imitator (who adopts the belief of others) is in a dilemma.
> The only muzzle of evil suggestions (of doubt) is Love. . . .
> O (dear) soul, Love alone cuts disputation short, for it (alone) comes to the rescue when you cry for help against arguments.[8]

Islam lays claim to the totality of the believer's life and thought.

[7] Abû Naṣr as-Sarrâj, *Kitâb al-luma' fî 't-taṣawwuf,* ed. R. A. Nicholson (Leyden and London, 1914), Nicholson's summary of p. 10 on p. iv of the Introduction.

[8] *Mathnawî,* ed. and trans. R. A. Nicholson (London, 1925-40), Book V, 3225, 3230a, 3240.

The community as the true repository of the living faith—there is no church organization that stands apart from the body of the lay faithful—is compelled to decide its political problems on religious grounds. The early sects doubtless owe their origin to deep-seated differences of outlook, religious and social, but they crystallized into communities within the general body of the Muslins under the impact of concrete political situations. The egalitarian and rigoristic Khârijites were drawn together by their dissent from the majority on the double questions of the legitimate ruler and of the proper authority to ascertain those qualifications in specific persons (A.D. 658). The Shî'ites, themselves destined to split into many groups, broke away when, through the assassination of 'Alî (A.D. 661) and the death in battle of his son, Ḥusain (A.D. 680), their desire for a caliph descended from the Prophet had been decisively frustrated. What had appeared to be a temporal issue—the quest for the rightful holder of the imamate, the leadership of the community—came to be the center of their theology. They revived the old motif of the epiphany of the divine in man and taught that the imam of necessity was a descendant of 'Alî, the Prophet's cousin and son-in-law, as the carrier of a particle of the divine light or substance was the indispensable guide to eternal bliss. And it would seem that the rise of the Mu'tazilite school was closely connected with the rise of the Abbasid dynasty (750-1258).

Majority Islam, usually called "Sunnite," has developed a rather limited concept of political authority. The Sunnite state is definitely not a welfare state, and it is not, like the Greek state, concerned with the happiness, *eudaimonia,* of its members.[9] The function of the Muslim state is well defined by Ghazzâlî when he explains that doubtless one of the purposes of the Lord was the good organization of the religious life. Now this organization is not attainable without an imam whose authority will be obeyed. Thus the imam and the state organization at his disposal have no other function than to make possible that life under God which the canon law has elaborated on the basis of authoritative text and tradition. The imam must therefore protect the territory of Islam from encroach-

[9] Cf., e.g., Plato, *Republic* 473 D-E, and, later, Justin Martyr (*First Apology* iii. 2, 3), who quotes the passage.

ment by unbelievers, or even extend it, and must domestically keep law and order so that the believer can practice his religious duties in safety. The caliph is the successor of Muḥammad as leader of the community; but, in his capacity as prophet and legislator, Muḥammad cannot have a successor. The caliph sees to it that the injunctions of the Prophet as interpreted by the orthodox jurisconsults are carried out, but he has no right to interpret them himself, let alone to add to or abrogate them. He will issue executive orders which have to be obeyed, he will impose taxes beyond those allowed by Revelation; but in a sense this activity will be tainted with illegality; it will be dangerous for the pious to get caught in administration and especially in the administration of justice. The canon-law judge, the *qâḍî,* will find himself unable to take care effectively of all contingencies; another type of court, that of "wrongs," *maẓâlim,* will be developed in which procedure is not bound by canon-law tradition and therefore is more readily adaptable to the conditions of the day. In almost every Islamic country there developed at one time or another the characteristic parallelism of law codes, one the unalterable *shar',* the cannon law in the systemization of one of the four recognized law schools, the other a code of "secular" origin, be it that of the conquering Mongols in Persia or a code arising gradually from custom and royal decisions, as in Egypt and Turkey. In practice the tendency has always been to confine the application of the *shar'* to matters of personal statute, so as to make the call for restoration of the *shar'* to full authority over all provinces of the legal life of the community a regular part of the program of conservative reformers.

The complete intertwining of the secular and the religious in a political issue becomes very real in the words which 'Alî addressed to his soldiers before the battle of Ṣiffîn (A.D. 657):

> Sacrifice yourselves! You are under the eyes of the Lord and with the cousin of His prophet. Renew your charge and disdain flight, for it will disgrace your offspring and mean the Fire for you on the Day of Reckoning. Before you are this great Sawâd [the fruitland of Iraq] and those large tents! Let blood flow profusely. For Satan is halting on his hill spreading out his two arms; he has stretched forth one hand for the assault and drawn back one foot to retreat, firmly implanted he will not budge until the truth manifests itself. But you will have

> the better of the struggle; God is with you and He will not allow you to lose [the merit] of your deeds.[10]

In contrast to the Sunnite rulers, the Shî'ite imams "are the mediators between God and mankind. Except by their intercession it is impossible for men to avoid the punishment of God." [11] The existence of an imam is not a matter of expediency, as is that of a Sunnite ruler; it is a metaphysical necessity. Mankind is in permanent need of guidance, and divine guidance is vouchsafed only through the sinless imam. From this it follows that the imam has legislative prerogatives. It does not follow, however, that the imam must be in power or even that he must be visible to the mass of mankind. In fact, for the majority of the Shî'ites the last historically traceable imam, Muḥammad Abû'l-Qâsim, removed himself from sight (in A.D. 879) but continues his spiritual function as the Hidden Imam, who at God's appointed time will return and openly take up the government of the world. The present rulers are but his stadholders, so to speak, whose authority derives from him. As late as 1906 the first constitution of Persia embodied the statement that parliament was to be established with the agreement and consent of the (Hidden) Imam of the Age.

There cannot be equality between those who have and those who spurn absolute truth. Muḥammad extended limited recognition to those religious groups that possessed a book, such as the Jews and Christians. The pagan was to be summoned to conversion or death; the scripturary was to remain outside the solidarity-circle of the ruling class unless he left his denomination voluntarily. Covenants affiliated the non-Muslim denominations to the Muslim state by according them autonomy in their internal affairs. Non-Muslims were liable to taxation beyond that imposable on Muslims, subjected to legalized social and professional discrimination, excluded from military service, and, in theory, barred from executive government office. They reproduced on a more parochial scale the organization of the Muslim state. This state came to harbor an increasing number of

[10] Mas'ûdî, *Murûj,* ed. Barbier de Meynard and Pavet de Courteille (Paris, 1861-77), IV, 355-56. Cf. the religious war cries of the Byzantine armies.

[11] Majlisî (d. 1699); quoted by D. M. Donaldson, *The Shî'ite Religion* (London, 1933), p. 344.

religiopolitical enclaves, owing to the tendency, already apparent in the late Roman and Byzantine empires, for unsuccessful sectarian movements to settle in an outlying province and organize as a semi-independent and statelike society.

Whether or not Muḥammad had in the course of his career come to envisage his mission as addressed to all mankind, the Muslim community did so interpret it. To spread the faith and to widen the Muslim-ruled territory was one of the principal duties of the caliph. The Law did not recognize the possibility of peace with the unbelievers, although expediency might require long periods of truce. But the task of extending the realm of truth on earth will not be fulfilled as long as non-Muslims remain in control of any part of this globe.

II

The tendencies inherent in the origins of Islam were to mature under the influence of those [contacts], in a sense . . . accidental, which grew out of the historical setting of the period, and, more specifically, the conquest by the Muslims of the high-civilization areas of Persia, Syria, and Egypt.

In assessing the Islamic achievement, it must be realized that the backwardness of the Arabian peninsula in relation to the cultural level of the neighboring countries made the early development of Islam largely a process of adjustment to the traditions of the older Near Eastern civilizations. The mental and political energy of the invaders prevented their absorption by the more numerous and more advanced subject peoples. Proselytism increased with the passing of time, and after four centuries Hither Asia (except for Byzantine territory) had become overwhelmingly Muslim. For some time conversion was politically and socially incomplete as long as it was not followed up by affiliation as a client with an Arab tribe, but gradually this uncanonic requirement lapsed and the non-Arabs became full-fledged Muslims in their own right.

Jewish and Christian thought-motifs had been instrumental in the formation of the Prophet's ideas; biblical and haggadic lore permeate the koranic narratives. His very monotheism was developed at least partially in controversy against Christian trinitarianism. But the way of life imposed by Muḥammad, the ritual of the pilgrimage, and, on the level of verbalization and argumentation, a certain prephilosophical crudeness—all this was genuinely Arab; and, with the pilgrimage anchored among the essentials of the faith and the Koran the permanent point of departure for theological thought, much of the Arab heritage has been preserved. It was not only the partial identification of Islam and Arabism through the development of Arabic into the representative language of Muslim civilization and the inalienable prestige of the Arabs as compatriots of the "Best of Mankind" and the rulers of the early empire which helped to keep an Arabic veneer on the composite culture of medieval (and modern) Islam. It was much rather the development of original forms of presentation like the *ḥadîth,* prophetic saying, with its witness-chain, *isnâd,* and text, *matn,* and its expansion into histories like the *Sîra* ("biography") of the Prophet by Ibn Isḥâq (d. 767) or the *Annals* of Ṭabarî (d. 923). And although on occasion the originality of the form may be questioned, the perfect acculturation is beyond doubt. The Muslim scholars sometimes voiced their consciousness of having appropriated foreign materials or foreign forms, but not a single borrowing proved effective, let alone lasting, unless Arabicized in terminology and cast into a familiar thought-pattern.

Acquaintance with Christian theology compelled the reluctant Muslims to overhaul and make explicit their faith in the terms of Greek thought-categories, a repetition of the process through which, some centuries earlier, Christianity had attained its intellectual elaboration. This developmental analogy constitutes one cause for that conspicuous unity of feeling and thinking in which East and West are tied, unconsciously for the most part, throughout the Middle Ages. Greek philosophy, especially Aristotelian and Neo-Platonic and, to a less[er] degree, Stoic, was studied intensively during the ninth and tenth centuries. But in philosophy as well as in less crucial fields, like literary theory, the age was not prepared to accept unadulterated Hellenism. The Islamic peripatetics, *falâsifa* (plural of *failasûf, philosophos*), always remained outside the pale as far as the feeling of the majority was concerned, while the Mu'tazila, although often decried as heretics, always "belonged," even as Qudâma's (d. 922) literary system, despite the clarity of its Greek-inspired categorization, never achieved the success which came to the less complete and fairly disorganized system of Ibn al-Mu'tazz (d. 908), who had been better able to Arabicize what he had learned from the classical masters.

The religious needs of the community, to which, in the last analysis, theology will have to bow, were barely touched by foreign ideas. The great dispute of the ninth century—the relation of God to his Book, a replica in one sense of the problem of the relation of the Logos to the Father and in another a special application of the problem of divine accidents—led to government intervention on the side of the Mu'tazila, who pronounced the Koran created by, and thus secondary to, God so as to avoid the "polytheistic" solution of positing two entities existing *ab aeterno.* Orthodoxy considered the Book as uncreate and coeval with Allâh. Popular sentiment was with the orthodox, and in due time the government yielded. The boundless reverence for the Book which had inspired orthodox arguments then came to express itself in the startling, but emotionally satisfying, absurdity of a doctrine which declared even the actual copy of the Book in the believer's hand and his actual recitation from it as uncreate. Greek thought, especially of the postclassical period, was better able to penetrate sectarian circles when the attempt was made to Islamicize Gnostic concepts toward the end of the millennium. But, while the formal framework and the logical tooling would be Hellenistic in a general sense, koranic and Islamic materials and associations would provide the factual or fictional core. Similarly, the Hellenization (largely through Syriac mediation) of mystical terminology and (in part) theory must have eluded the pious, owing to its perfect integration in the traditional language of devotion.

In the sphere of scientific activities, on the other hand, the consciousness of a definite distinction between indigenous and foreign sciences never disappeared, however much the Muslim scholars might have made their own and added to the classical bequest. The native or Arabic sciences explored essentially religion and language, branching out into koranic exegesis, koranic criticism (i.e., the study of the readings of the text, the science of Tradition (*ḥadîth*), jurisprudence, and scholastic theology; and grammar, lexicography, rhetoric, and literature, respectively. The foreign sciences, *'ulûm al-awâ'il* (literally, "the sciences of the ancients"), were defined by the Spaniard, Ibn Ṭumlûs (d. 1223), as those common to all peoples and religious communities, as opposed to such sciences as had been peculiarly developed by Islam. They are primarily the propaedeutic, physical, and metaphysical sciences of the Greeks: the various branches of mathematics, philosophy, natural history (zoology, botany, etc.), medicine, astronomy, music, magic, and alchemy.

The study of these foreign sciences, however intense and fruitful, never fought clear of a measure of distrust on the part of the pious. In fact, the animosity toward these studies increased in the later Middle Ages, and there can be little doubt that the hostility was called forth not only by the subject matter but also by the foreign and non-Muslim authorities on which they largely relied. The pious is to avoid any science that might endanger his faith. He is to heed the fundamental division of the sciences, not as foreign and native, but as (religiously) praiseworthy and blameworthy. All sciences are blameworthy that are useless for this or the other world. The Prophet is alleged to have prayed to God to protect him against useless knowledge. Orthodox theology inclined toward an interpretation of "useful" as necessary or helpful for the practice of religion, *'amal.* In this manner two semi-independent strands of intellectual effort were cultivated side by side, with the ancient sciences slowly losing out in the perpetual struggle between the theological and the philosophical-scientific approach.

The civil wars shifted the political center of the Empire from Arabia, first to Syria and then (ca. A.D. 750) to Iraq. The Abbasid rulers in Baghdad carried through what might be called the transformation of the state from the patrimonial to the "rational" stage, a process that had already been started toward the end of the Syrian period. The administration was stabilized on the Sassanian model, the number of government bureaus increased, their functions were more clearly defined, and chancellery procedure was meticulously regulated. In the tenth century the administration of the caliph worked through about a dozen central boards, *dîwâns,* such as the War Office, the Board of Expenditure (mostly concerned with the requirements of the court), the State Treasury, the Dispatch Board, and the General Post Office (which also discharged the duties of the secret police). The vizier presided over the heads of the individual *dîwâns*. The provinces that were represented in the capital by managing boards were governed by an army commander together with a chief of the civil administration, whose main function was taxgathering. It was usually the first step to local independence when both offices were intrusted to the same person. The annual budget was carefully worked out, and the growth of the appropriation for the court at the expense of public services, such as maintenance of border fortifications or road-building, in the tenth century mirrors the decline of the empire and some of its causes. The chancellery was staffed by literary men, who in their relation to the court played a role comparable to that of the humanists in the bureaus of Western states during the Renaissance.

By and large, Islam had been able to win the first loyalty of the masses, but it was unable to eliminate nationalism as a social and political force. The non-Arab nations compensated for their depressed status by playing up their cultural accomplishments and the deeds of their ancestors. They reproached the Arabs for their barbarous manners and customs and raked up tribal scandals with a view to casting doubts on that paramount pride of the Arab, his genealogy. The Arabs struck back, particularly after Persian influence at the Abbasid court had come to outweigh theirs, basing their claim to superiority above all on their kinship with the Messenger of God, and then on the unexcelled richness of their language and the matchless beauties of their poetry. The level of these discussions is somewhat childish but not much more so than that of similar contests between Greeks and barbarians regarding their respective contributions to civilization in the Hellenistic age.

The political breakup that began in the eighth but really became acute only in the ninth and tenth centuries mostly followed national lines. Spain, Berber North Africa, and Egypt in the West and the Iranian countries in the East regained their independence, *de facto* or *de jure;* even within the Arabic-speaking territory of Syria, Iraq, and the peninsula the regional interests reasserted themselves. This breakup added Cairo and Cordova to the centers of Arabic-Islamic civilization. It was never completely repaired, but it did not impair the cultural coherence of the region. Scholars traveled freely throughout the Islamic world, statesmen passed easily from the service of one prince into that of another. Common faith and common education overrode political divisions. Political and denominational, national and social affiliations overlapped. The sects were international but usually had a localized political base and connections with definite strata of society, like that of the extreme Shî'a with the artisan guilds. Sunnite Islam was very slow to exclude dissenters. The Prophet was quoted as saying that the difference of opinion within the community was a mercy from the Lord, and as indicating that Islam would see the growth of seventy-three sects, all but one of which would be on the right path. The theologians, although hesitant when it comes to the precise definition of those to be excommunicated, are more rigorous than popular sentiment. The sects are by nature exclusive and likely to recognize true believership only in their own members. Ghazzâlî bars the *falâsifa* from the community. He feels uncertain about Mu'tazilites, anthropomorphists, and "the other sects," as their errors are shaded delicately and are compensated by their holding correct beliefs in some respects. The only rule which in his view is established by the Koran is that the denier of the Prophet must be excommunicated. (This discussion must be understood in the light of the fact that there does not exist in Islam a body whose decision would be binding on all Muslims, although in specific cases a body of theologians may authorize the government to spill the blood of a defendant who has been found to harbor heretical tenets.) Of such dissenters as were not implicated in revolutionary movements it would seem that pantheistic philosophers were the most likely victims of persecution.

III

In every age self-expression is limited in part by convention that compels the speaker or writer to dwell on some, and disregard other, aspects of his experience, and in part by the heritage of forms and imagery of which the individual may dispose.

Arabic literature, like Greek and Roman, is very conscious of the peculiar requirements of the several kinds, but its repertory of kinds is considerably smaller than that of classical antiquity. Of the three basic genres which antiquity developed, drama and epic are absent. Poetry rates higher than prose (an occasional dissenting theorist notwithstanding) because it demands the greater skill. The ability to master the intricacies of prosody and the formal rules binding the various types of poetry attracts the admiration of the public. The public and, even more, the average critic, who as a rule started out as a grammarian and lexicographer, insist on the maintenance of traditional norms—the ode, *qaṣîda,* must begin with reflections on bygone love and preferably refer to the scene of his love, now forsaken; the poet must profess to seek comfort by mounting a magnificent camel for a perilous ride through the desert; and he must conclude by addressing a request to a high-placed personality or by praising his tribe (or himself) or acting as spokesman for his group on some political issue. The classical, i.e., pagan, tradition remained the strongest single strain in Arabic poetry throughout the Middle Ages, and down to the beginning of the twentieth century, although Persian (e.g., introduction of new meters and the banqueting song) and Hellenistic influences (e.g., new attitudes in love and poetry) were absorbed readily enough.

The real centers of pre-Islamic civilization were urban settlements, but its literature was dedicated to the glorification of Bedouin ideals. The authority accorded it kept an incongruous note of desert lyrics in Islamic poetry. The early Abbasid age witnessed a remarkable efflorescence of poetical achievement. Modes were found to capture the colorful gaiety of the court, the moralizing sentiment of the repenting libertine, and that subtilized and worshipful love which was destined to pass through Spain into the songs of the Troubadours, along with some of the complicated prosodical forms of which the Spanish Arabs were fond. Modernistic poets toyed with new meters of lighter rhythm, while the conservatives used the inherited framework for a display of verbal virtuosity. Under the patronage of the courts and the dignitaries of the empire, the poet became the mouthpiece of the political powers; his economic and social status rose in many instances, but poetry lost what the poets may have gained. Reckless eulogizing and equally reckless lampooning, the need to outdo the predecessor and the rival in giving vent to the same kind of sentiments and aspirations, accompanied by a taste which confined the poet to a limited body of subject matter and which applauded originality in the successful recasting of the familiar motif—this combination of trends led to the increasing paralysis of creativeness and to the slowly dulling sparkle of verbal *tours de force* that is so characteristic of the poetry of the later Middle Ages. Only mysticism preserved its productive independence by providing the poet with an experience too strong to be fully dominated by convention. Here the danger was not traditionalism but abstruseness.

The impressionistic taste of the Arab is reflected in his insistence on the perfection of the individual verse rather than the composition of the whole; in prose, in his preference for anecdote and sketch instead of extended narrative; only popular prose exceeds moderate length but its tales consist of a collection of semicoherent episodes. Consistently planned and carefully executed composition appears to be the prerogative of the Persians, who developed a tradition of historical writing and even greater tradition of epic representation, with their own history, romance, and mysticism providing successively the subjects most favored by the public. The Persians, who also developed a religious drama centering on the death of Ḥusain at Kerbela (A.D. 680), surpassed the Arabs in creative imagination, perhaps also in a willingness to abandon themselves to the intoxicating associations of figurative and symbolic speech. Fundamentally, however, their taste was the taste of the Arabs; and, on the whole, the literary taste of Islam parelleled that of the medieval West—in its submission to formal tradition, its intellectualization, its learned character, its emphasis on technique, its predilection for "gold and glitter" and for description in general, and most of all in its craving for *gharâba, curiositas,* the startling, the strange, and the unusual. The Muslim poet wishes to astound the hearer. As in the European *secentismo,* his *concetti* are meant to induce a feeling of wonderment and surprise, of *maraviglia, 'ajab.* What imagery and witticism are supposed to effect in poetry, digressions, the insertion of *mirabilia,* and rapid shifts from subject to subject will do in prose. The flagging of the reader's attention is to be avoided by every means, and it seems that the reader was unwilling to concentrate on one theme for a prolonged period of time; so episodic distraction and the near-destruction of coherent composition appeared imperative even to some of the greatest litterateurs.

The conquest of subject matter through a deepening of the psychological interest in man was successful only in the unreflected presentation of persons and incidents, in which again the authors of the ninth and tenth centuries excelled. However, a certain discretion, which is still characteristic of the Muslim manner, has prevented the literary analysis of the human soul and with it the rise of a psychologically adequate biography in the Greek and modern sense of the word. This is true in spite of the fact that the collections of biographies which Islam has produced are amazing achievements as regards the accumulation of material and that the Western Middle Ages have nothing remotely comparable to offer. The Muslim writer is a keen observer of emotions, but he confines his portrayal of them to the religious tract or the autobiographical description of conversion and perhaps the historical anecdote. Only devotional poetry benefitted.

Scholarship (outside the natural sciences), which went through a renascence in the fourteenth and fifteenth centuries, better preserved its insistence on the creative contribution but, at the same time, adapted its requirements to cover the majority of the works of the declining age. 'Almawî (d. 1573) quotes an earlier authority for this statement:

> Literary activity has seven subdivisions: (1) the creation of something new. (2) The correction of the shortcomings which exist in a particular work. (3) The indication of the various mistakes (found in a particular work). (4) The explanation of difficulties which excessive brevity has caused in a particular work. (5) The shortening of tedious lengthy passages, without complicating the understanding of the whole work. (6) The proper arrangement of badly arranged material in a manner which would as little as possible disturb (the original arrangement). And (7) the proper arrangement of materials which were badly arranged in the work of a predecessor, in an intelligent manner which would make the new work more suitable for didactic purposes.[12]

Pre-Islamic Arabia's contribution to the arts did not go beyond her achievement in poetry. There was no native tradition in the fine arts on which Islam could build. So "art in Islamic countries is a derivative of the classical traditions followed in various Oriental

[12] Trans. F. Rosenthal, *The Technique and Approach of Muslim Scholarship* (Rome, 1947), pp. 64-5.

countries preceding the Arab conquest. Sometimes this influence is rather pure and direct; in other cases the influence came by way of Sassanian and Coptic art. There are also extraneous influences, such as those from India." [13]

The austerity which Islam in its ceremonial aspects never lost denied to craftsmanship the incentive of working precious metals for mosque treasuries and put a brake on architectural exuberance. The mosque is originally a bare and simply articulated building; in the Arab countries an open court with fountains for the ritual ablutions is usually larger than the mosque proper. A tower from which the call to prayer is sounded adds a striking feature to the complex of buildings. The walls of the interior, unless they remain simply whitewashed, are decorated with ornamentalized script-bands of koranic verses and the names of the Prophet and his "well-guided" successors. Often the script is placed on enameled tiles, whose soft colors and designs tend to relieve the harsh calm of the empty hall without narrowing it down. The age-old aversion to pictorial representation of living beings which has asserted itself in Hither Asia in several periods within different civilizations has in Islam crystallized in the much-quoted saying attributed to the Prophet that the artist will be asked on Judgment Day to breathe life into the figures he wrought and that he will be condemned to the Fire if unable to do so. Since there were no saints in early and in official Islam, painting in any case would have had to concentrate on worldly subjects. Departure from lifelikeness was the device that the Islamic artist used to avoid the presumption of "creating" living beings. The book-painter, especially the Persian, did not shy away from portraying scenes of Muslim history and of the life of Muḥammad, even venturing at times to picture the Prophet himself. But, in spite of the superb development of miniaturing, the religiously sanctioned prejudice stunted the growth of painting and completely barred sculpture. Architecture and the so-called "minor arts," prominently including calligraphy, remained the principal areas in which the Islamic artist was able to express himself. Decoration largely took the place of representation. A *horror vacui* caused every available space on wall, manuscript, or vase and

[13] R. Ettinghausen, in *The Arab Heritage,* ed. N. A. Faris (Princeton, 1944) p. 251.

platter to be covered with luxuriant, laboriously interlaced ornaments, in which end merges into beginning, fragments of Scripture into lineaments without rational meaning. The fully decorated mosque is still austere, but no longer simple. The ornament is designed to blur the clarity of the architectural plan. In taste and intent Islamic art is as far removed from its classical inspiration as is Islamic poetry from the classical inspiration of its theory.

IV

This world is no more than a proving ground on which man prepares for the final judgment. It will surely come to an end, and the signs by which mankind will know its approach have been revealed in many an eschatological tradition. History is restricted to a comparatively short period. If it is to be told as far as unfolded, the tale must begin with Creation and record the revelations accorded to the several peoples and tell of the rise and decline of kings and empires in the shadow of God's favor and God's wrath. With Muḥammad the beginning of the last phase is reached, and before too long the prelude to eternity will have died away. Imbedded between two metaphysical pivots, Creation and Judgment, man's life in history is but an episode whose true cause in God's essence or will remains inscrutable. Nevertheless, the Muslim evinces great interest in the events that take up this episode. He is fascinated with man's actions, and he is a keen and accurate recorder. The enormous collections of materials which Islamic civilization has produced tend to personalize the historical process, to avoid delving into underlying causes and seeking for a comprehensive analysis and interpretation of historical forces. There was profound understanding of the mechanics of political growth and disintegration, but only occasional attention was given to the social and economic background and the reason for the appeal of ideologies. Some slight and puzzling evidence could perhaps be adduced for the existence of an undercurrent of philosophical history. What is certain, however, is a strong interest in political theory or perhaps in a peculiar combination of political science as the systematic description of government and political theory as its normative doctrine. This is to say that Islam is lacking in a comparative study of constitutions, that it was not inclined to investigate the operation of the state in the abstract, and that it remained completely uninterested in the forms of political life that had developed outside Muslim civilization. The description of the functioning of the Muslim state is most adequate when it comes to the detail of its judicial and executive administration. In the presentation of the role of the caliph, one senses the uneasy efforts of the author to harmonize the ideal task and the humble facts of his period. The Law has laid down unalterable principles, never envisaging the increasing incapacity of the Prince of the Believers to exercise even his more modest duties. So theory is compelled to compromise, to stretch the concept of election to include election by one qualified voter—in other words, to sanction the actual situation in which the caliph is appointed by his predecessor or the military leader who happens to be in control. Even the possibility of a plurality of leaders of the community has to be admitted. As in other ages and other civilizations, the theory of power comes to be a weapon in the fight for power.

Too late to influence Islamic thought but in time to exploit the political and cultural experience of the Muslim West before its downfall in Spain and its intellectual ruin in North Africa, Ibn Khaldûn, statesman, judge, and historian (d. 1406), attempted an interpretation of the processes of history. History, he explains at the beginning of his celebrated *Prolegomena* to his *Universal History,* is one of the branches of knowledge which are handed on from people to people and generation to generation; it is attractive even to the lowly and is eagerly sought after by the kings and equally appreciated by lettered and unlettered. Outwardly, it seeks to retrace the happenings that have marked past centuries and empires. It attracts by telling of the changes that people have undergone and of the deeds done by the divers nation ere they were summoned off the stage. In its essence, *bâṭin,* history is examination and verification of facts, exact investigation into their causes, profound knowledge of how events happened and what their origin was. Thus history emerges as an important branch of philosophy.

On the basis of source criticism, whose guiding principle is to measure the past by the present and to reject what experience shows to be impossible now, Ibn Khaldûn arrives at a thorough analysis of the political organism; and he presents his results with equal emphasis on psychological and historical fact. He lays bare the life-cycle of empires from nomadism through conquest and subsequent corruption in urban life to decline and displacement from power. Civilization presupposes urbanism, but city life leads to degeneracy, and the quest for an improved existence draws ever new waves of barbarian nomads into the eddy of acculturation, where their passionate solidarity feeling cools off, their cohesion weakens, and the very physical basis of their power is corroded. Three or perhaps four generations suffice to turn the wheel full circle.

This neutral thesis is Islamicized by the recognition of the function of prophecy; for within the historical process man seeks salvation quite independently of the fate of his society. And it is the prophets whom God "has made to be means of access between Him and His creatures, that they may instruct men as to what is best for them, and may exhort them to accept their guidance, and may keep them from the Fire, and guide them in the way of Salvation." [14] A religious bond like the adherence to the same prophetic revelation will create the strongest possible solidarity feelings, so that groups united and prompted to aggressive action by a religious impulse will be most likely to enter successfully the cycle of empire-building.

Unless he were to reject it, the Muslim philosopher had to justify Revelation in the light of natural reason or else to appraise reason by weighing its conclusions against the insights conveyed by the Koran. To test the means of cognition by each other and to ascertain their compatibility or their complementary character may have seemed a work of piety to the philosopher but actually was an encroachment on the autonomy of Revelation and a switch to anthropocentrism, even if the result was a refusal to recognize two independent truths based, respectively, on faith and on reason. When Ibn Ṭufail (d. 1185), the contemporary and compatriot of Averroës (d. 1198), demonstrates in his tale of *Ḥayy b. Yaqẓân* ("Alive, the Son of Awake") that an isolated human being by con-

[14] Cairo edition, n.d. p. 91; Trans. D. B. MacDonald, *The Religious Attitude and Life in Islam* (Chicago, 1909), p. 43.

sidering "philosophically" the world about him could, guided by reason alone, arrive at the verities guaranteed by Revelation, he not only brings down Revelation to the human level but voices a prouder view of man's potentialities than could be acceptable to the theologians. To conceive of Revelation as systematizing and verifying the fundamental truths deducible from reasoned experience will deprive the incidental, the factual-historical, even much of the legal, content of the Book of its significance. As society largely depends for its organization on this concrete and philosophically less relevant part of Revelation, philosophy will have to become esoteric in order to eschew a hopeless conflict. When Ḥayy toward the end of his life is found by the vizier of the neighboring king, he sails to the king's island to preach the pure faith but soon returns, having realized that the multitude demands a sensuous adumbration of the truth rather than the truth itself. In the light of history, the tale—an elaboration of an idea of Avicenna (d. 1037), and probably one of the sources of Defoe's *Robinson Crusoe*—comes to symbolize the state of Muslim civilization as the Middle Ages draw to a close. Philosophy reaches out far and high but is denied efficacy in its own society as Islam hardens and contracts to remain intact in the face of recession. The insights of the esoterics, smaller and smaller enclaves within a resurgent and zealous orthodoxy, and especially Averroës' conception of Aristotelianism, are opened by translation to the West, but put out of sight, not to say forgotten, in the East.

Every civilization and every age favor a limited number of human types for whom they will provide the fullest means of self-realization, while denying it to an even larger number for whose peculiar gifts the prevailing pattern affords no socially meaningful use. The athlete and the rhetor, idolized in antiquity, are unknown in Islam; the peasant, idealized by romanticism as the repository of genuine folk culture, is held in low esteem by Islam and never attracts the attention of the learned. Islam prefers the sedentary to the nomad, the city-dweller to the villager. It accepts the artisan but respects the merchant. The sword ranks lower than the pen. Religious knowledge is more desirable than wealth. Outside the circles of the canon lawyers, gnosis comes to be rated above rational knowledge. The prophet as the ideal head of the hierarchy, the mystic saint, the visionary, the ascetic (whose abstention does not, as a rule, include sexual self-denial), on the one hand, the scholar, the jurist-theologian, and the litterateur, on the other, are encouraged by this civilization. Power is fascinating and awesome but transient, the king and the officials a disturbing body in the peace-loving but war-ridden, industrious, and exploited community.

The prevailing attitude toward power is skepticism. The caliph 'Umar ([reigned] 634-644) begins a letter to his governor at Baṣra with the words: "People have an aversion from their rulers, and I trust to Allah that you and I are not overtaken by it, stealthily and unexpectedly, or by hatreds conceived against us." [15] As an executive officer, the ruler is unrestricted. The absoluteness of his power was never challenged. The Muslim liked his rulers terror-inspiring, and it seems to have been *bon ton* to profess one's self awe-struck when ushered into their presence. "For in the grades of existence and the ranks of the intelligibles, after the Prophetic function, which is the supreme limit of man's attainment, there is no rank higher than kingship, which is naught else than a Divine gift." [16] Ibn aṭ-Ṭiqṭaqà wrote in 1302:

> Know that a king has attributes peculiar to himself, which distinguish him from the commons. Amongst them is the fact that, when he likes a thing, the people like it, and when he dislikes a thing, the people dislike it, either naturally or so pretending thereby to curry favor with him. Hence the saying, "The people follow the faith of their rulers." . . . Another attribute peculiar to the ruler is that when he shows aversion from a man that man becomes faint-hearted, even though undamaged by him, and when he approaches a man that man is encouraged, even though unbenefited by him. Plain aversion or approach achieves that, and only a ruler has that attribute.[17]

The caliph Ma'mûn (813-33) is quoted as saying: "The best life has he who has an ample house, a beautiful wife, and sufficient means, who does not know us, and whom we do not know."

The medieval Muslim is not a citizen in the Greek or the post-

[15] R. Levy, *Sociology of Islam* (London, 1931), I, 283-84.

[16] Nizâmî 'Arûdi (fl. 1110-52), *Chahâr Maqâla,* trans. E. G. Browne (London, 1921), p. 3.

[17] Ibn aṭ-Ṭiqṭaqà, *Kitâb al-Fakhrî,* trans. C. E. J. Whitting (London, 1947), pp. 22-3.

Renaissance sense of the word. The vicissitudes of government are his concern only when faith is at war with unbelief. He assumes no responsibility for social or civic betterment beyond defraying his canonical obligations to the authorities and his fellow-men. He is frequently impatient with his rulers, and thinks little of rioting, but on the whole he is content to let the princes play their game. During the reign of the Flavians (A.D. 70-96), Apollonius of Tyana was accused by some of influencing the young to lead a retired life, and the same reproach was hurled against the Christians, but no Muslim ever was rebuked for damaging the civic spirit. No Muslim government ever tried to develop civic sentiment. Accordingly, there was little attachment to the political body to which one happened to belong or for any particular regime (except on sectarian grounds). But there was an overwhelming feeling for the oneness of the Muslim community and a realization that any political sacrifice was justified to enable the community to continue under the Law as far as possible. Ghazzâlî says:

> There are those who hold that the imamate is dead, lacking as it does the required qualifications. But no substitute can be found for it. What then? Are we to give up obeying the law? Shall we dismiss the *qâḍîs,* declare all authority to be valueless, cease marrying and pronounce the acts of those in high places to be invalid at all points, leaving the populace to live in sinfulness? Or shall we continue as we are, recognizing that the imamate really exists and that all acts of the administration are valid, given the circumstances of the case and the necessities of the actual moment.[18]

The education of the non-theologian centered on literature and, broadly speaking, the humanities in general. Grammatical, philosophical, and historical questions were assured of wide interest. The relative rank of the major poets was hotly argued. The demand for *polymathia,* together with the accelerating accumulation of material in all fields, created the need for scientific encyclopedias as well as for encyclopedias of the gentleman's knowledge that treated their subjects with the aid of illustrative verse, anecdotes, and apothegms, provided the reader with quotable phrases, and attempted to instruct while entertaining. Ibn Qutaiba (d. 889), the author of the

[18] Levy, *op. cit.,* p. 306.

'Uyûn al-akhbâr, or "Sources of Information," one of the earliest specimens of the literary encyclopedia, devotes its ten sections to discussions of government, war, nobility, natural disposition, and character; learning and scholars; asceticism; social relations; human needs of all kinds; food; and women. He explains that he has dealt in separate books with drinks, the basic data of the sciences, poetry, and the interpretation of dreams. This is how Ibn Qutaiba characterizes the contents of the first section of the *'Uyûn:*

> It contains the narratives about the station of government, the differences of its circumstances, its mode of life, the deportment the ruler stands in need of with regard to his companions; about his addresses, his transactions, his consultations; the principles he has to adhere to in selecting his officials, judges, chamberlains, scribes, and governors, in order that they may follow his ways in their decisions. It also contains curious sayings and verses appropriate to these narratives.

The whole work he has composed as "an eye-opener for the learned, as an education for the leaders of men and those whom they lead, as a place for the kings to rest in from the toil of endeavor and weariness." [19]

When about one hundred years later the vizier Ibn Sa'dân (in office 983/4-985/6) asks the great litterateur Abû Ḥayyân at-Tauḥîdî (d. 1009) to spend his evenings in his company, they discuss such subjects as the condition of man, the nature of the soul, the character of important contemporaries, the outstanding qualities of the Arabs as compared to other nationalities, the relative usefulness to the ruler of accountancy and stylistics, and the superiority of grammar over logic. At a later period mysticism would probably have figured prominently in their conversations.

V

As in its rise the political configuration of the period became significant only through the willingness of Islam to respond, so in its decline did the barbarian invasions and usurpations succeed only because of the waning devotion to its original political ideal. The concept of the caliph as God's trustee and as the guarantor of a com-

[19] Trans. J. Horovitz, *Islamic Culture,* IV (1930), 180, 174.

munity life under God had ceased to rouse and rally the Muslims long before the Mongols conquered Baghdad and executed the last Abbasid caliph (A.D. 1258). Outside of Persia, which they never subjugated, the population was only mildly interested when the Ottoman Turks displaced their rulers, who had for some time been mostly foreigners with more than a touch of the robber-baron.

During the great age of Islam, Greek philosophy and Greek science had battered the walls of orthodoxy. Every advance in thought, in insight into the ways of nature, every effort devoted to acculturating and developing the offerings of classical antiquity, was at the very least energy withdrawn from the Law and pressure brought to bear on theology to catch up with the intellectual climate of the period so as to justify itself before the intellectual leadership.

While orthodoxy might take comfort in the realization that the Hellenized intelligentsia was small in numbers and without a real footing among the mass of the believers, the sectarian movements were clearly popular revolts. Economic stress, social injustice, and the appeal of the Shî'ite ideology in its integration into Islam of pre-Islamic—Gnostic and ancient Near Eastern—ideas had put the Sunnite government on the defensive as early as the end of the ninth century. By the end of the eleventh the political situation of orthodoxy had become precarious. Emotionally it lost its hold as the Sûfîs emerged more and more as the bearers of the true religious life of the community. Ṣûfism had become the repository of the religious psychology of Islam, and its analysis of the religious life the timeless enrichment of human self-interpretation and the most delicate crystallization of the Muslim's spiritual aspirations. Dogmatically dangerous for its tendency toward a *unio spiritualis* between God and man, toward the ecstatic realization of a commingling of substances, divine and human, it was even more dangerous to the community by its implicit antinomianism—if the Law is not needed for union, why observe it after union has been attained? The quietist attitude of the mystics strengthened the antipolitical outlook of the faithful. Mysticism, as it had come to be the real religion of the Muslim world, gave final approval to that aversion from the political life and from civic education, to that defective, because actionless, humanism which is far and away the most important single cause of the decay of Islamic civilization.

Orthodoxy finally mastered its crisis. The Crusades ended sectarian expansion. The Ayyubids gave Egypt after two hundred years its first Sunnite government (A.D. 1171). Heterodox Persia broke away politically from the Arabic-speaking world. Defeats and calamities drew the people closer to tradition. The perfecting of scholasticism safeguarded the orthodox position in theology. The decomposing stimulus of Greek thought seemed no longer needed when its methodological contribution had been absorbed. The sciences receded under suspicion of heresy. The governments made ready to lend their arm to the orthodox reaction and assisted it through education and repression. What had been the caution of traditionalism became the rigor of fear and soon of death. The period knew that it was sterile and declining. Literary formalism and intellectual rigidity were to accommodate the unlettered, accompanied by hospitality to pre-Islamic popular beliefs, to the demoniacal world of Hellenistic magic as well as the worship of the Ṣûfî saints. The theologians of the eleventh century, above all Ghazzâlî, secured Ṣûfism its place within orthodoxy. The Ṣûfî yielded his antinomianism and accepted a definition of union that ruled out consubstantiality of man and God; the orthodox spiritualized ritual worship along the lines of mystic experience. The emotive life of Sunnite Islam came to be concentrated in the Ṣûfî orders.

The Turkish conquest (completed early in the sixteenth century) stabilized the political situation of the Near East. It cut off most of the Islamic area from Europe. Simultaneously, the shift of commerce from the Mediterranean to the Atlantic sealed the economic decline of the area that had, however, set in before the age of discoveries had reduced the value of the Muslim merchant's monopoly on the carrying trade between India and the West. One outburst of reforming primitivism, the Wahhâbî movement (from the middle of the eighteenth century), broke the quiet of a sleepy age. The Arab countries especially that had been the center of Muslim civilization submitted apathetically to the twin domination of orthodoxy and the Turks. It was only with Napoleon's expedition to Egypt (in 1798) that, through the impact of Europe and the rise of local nationalisms in its wake, Muslim civilization regained the willingness to change, to experiment, to risk—in short, to live.

3

PERSIA AND THE ARABS

Ruben Levy

An exact assessment of what the Arab world owes to Persia would demand an analysis of the civilizations of both, with digressions that might lead into the fathomless deeps of anthropology. Nevertheless, there are certain elements in the one which may be said, with an approach to historical truth, to have been derived from the other. In general they are superficial features, capable of statement as concrete facts. Of the imponderables which the two have interchanged only a little need or can be said here, for there is already a considerable literature on the subject.

The speed of the Muslim Arab subjugation of Persia has often been the object of comment, yet the matter is not as simple as appears in the bald assertion that the Arabs overran and absorbed the empire of the Sassanian Shahs. Persia did not then, or at any time, lose the identity which she had possessed almost from the beginnings of recorded history. The features making for her endurance were, of course, largely physical and geographical, but they consisted also in certain resilient and indestructible elements in the character of her people and their collective institutions. They remained identifiable even in the systems imposed by the Arabs, the conquerors who in historical times had left the greatest impress on the country.

As in the Moorish conquest of Spain, the flood of invasion did

Reprinted from *The Legacy of Persia*, ed. A. J. Arberry (Oxford, 1953). Reprinted by permission of the Clarendon Press, Oxford.

not cover the whole of Persia in one tide, but the rapidity and ease with which it submerged the main provinces may be attributed to the fact that the Arabs were not altogether unfamiliar to the Persians and that both peoples shared ancient religious and spiritual concepts. This becomes more obvious if comparison is made with the difficulties the Arabs encountered in their conflict with the Byzantine Empire. Especially in Iraq, the ancient Babylonia, which, though a province of the Sassanian Empire, was occupied by "Nabataeans," a people speaking a Semitic tongue, there had for long been fairly intimate contacts between Arabs and Persians. It was the kind of common ground lacking for Arab and Greek.

At the time of their Islam-inspired migration from their desert peninsula the Arabs were at a primitive level of military development, except for their skill in storming fortifications, owed possibly to the adoption of siege-engines from the Greeks. In the arts of peace too they had scarcely advanced beyond the stage of providing themselves with the prime necessities of life. The great mass of desert-dwellers indeed required no more than they could get from their camels, the only beasts able to thrive in the Arabian wilderness. Agriculture they held to be an occupation beneath the dignity of men and those who engaged in it mere clod-hoppers; from which it was only a step to the disregard of land itself as something outside the range of notice. In general they had little concern with the complexities and refinements of a settled existence.

Yet once the Arabs had burst into the open world beyond their peninsula, their leaders were faced with the necessity of administering their newly acquired possessions and hence of taking an interest in the unfamiliar art of government. The *Fakhrī,* an early-fourteenth-century manual of politics and history, relates how the caliph 'Umar, when at his wits' end to know how to distribute the spoils of war which were pouring in, sought the advice of a Persian who had once been employed in a government office. His suggestion was that a *dīvān,* a register or bureau, should be instituted for controlling income and expenditure, and this became the germ out of which grew the governmental machine that served the caliphate for some hundreds of years. The story contains a grain of truth, for perhaps the most important acquisition made by the Arabs was Madā'in (Seleucia-Ctesiphon) on the Tigris, the capital of the Sassanian Empire and the center of its administration and, at the same time, a city rivaling Constantinople for wealth and its civilized amenities. From it Kufa and Basra, Iraqi cities which had developed out of Arab military settlements, recruited the officials able to carry on the administration of the new territories in the early stages of their occupation, and incidentally to teach the tribesmen something of the business of government.

Amongst the leaders in the Arab world the Sassanian kings had long possessed a fabulous reputation for statesmanship. The ninth-century essayist Jāḥiẓ, of Basra gives expression to it when, in the course of an essay dealing with the qualities of the Turks, he indulges in a characteristic digression to air his views on sundry other peoples. "Amongst the races and generations of mankind," he says, "I have found that some excelled in the practical arts, some in rhetoric, some in the creation of empires and some in military skill." He goes on to say that his researches convinced him that the Greeks had a genius for philosophy and mechanical devices, that the Chinese were the most skilled artists as craftsmen without being greatly interested in the metaphysical causes of phenomena, and that the Turks were doughty warriors. As for the desert Arabs, they had never been merchants, tradesmen, or physicians nor had they any aptitude for mathematics or agriculture. On the other hand, when they gave their minds to poetry and oratory, to horses, weapons, and implements of war or to the recording of traditions and annals, they were unexcelled. "Of course," he adds, a regard for fact compelling him to qualify his generalizations, "not every Turk is a warrior nor every Arab a poet." Lastly, coming to the Persians, he awards the palm of statesmanship to the Sassanian Shahs.

Jāḥiẓ was merely corroborating the opinion of the caliphs. The Omayyad Hishām ibn 'Abd al-Malik (d. 743) had amongst his books an Arabic translation, made in his lifetime, of a Persian history of the Sassanians, illustrated with their portraits in "rare" colors and containing chapters on their political methods, the Persian sciences, and the chief monuments of the national architecture. Presumably the Persian system of government was the subject of his study; it was without a doubt closely followed by the Abbasid caliphs, for to Arabs it presented features that were strange and possibly unacceptable. One was that of an absolute, hereditary monarchy and another that of a government which was, in theory at any rate, strictly centralized. The Arabs, even in such cities as Mecca and Medina, grouped themselves in jealously independent tribes, each of which elected its own chief. Tribes might be divided and subdivided, but in none except the smallest unit was the headship ever hereditary, though it remained by tradition within certain designated families. Early in the history of Islam, in fact, sovereignty was declared to be outside the category of hereditable human possessions.

When the time came for the caliph 'Umar to organize the Muslim state, he provided for a sovereign ruler but retained the principle of election, though only members of the Prophet's tribe of the Quraish were eligible. Within the state the Arab conquerors were to hold a privileged position corresponding to that held in the Sassanian state by the nobly-born Iranian families. 'Umar himself and his three immediate successors in the caliphate were, in fact, elected to office, but Mu'āwīya, who followed them as first of the Omayyad caliphs, was able to create a family dynasty in which power descended from father to son, with an occasional deflexion to brother or cousin.

Apart from the sovereignty, 'Umar's administration bears the impress of the Persian system. Over the various newly acquired territories he placed his own agents, granting them certain restricted powers but keeping the final control in his own hands. The great landlords, who had acknowledged the later Sassanians only to the extent of submitting to taxation, were swept away, but the *dihqāns,* the more substantial peasantry whom the Sassanians had employed as minor revenue officials, were kept where they were to be the new government's assessment-officers and tax-gatherers. Substantially they were regarded much as the Arab notables in the various districts of Iraq were by the British forces who invaded that Turkish province in 1914. As being conversant with revenue conditions in their own district they were assigned certain functions in connection with them. It was the *dihqāns* who kept the taxation registers and could say from experience what the various revenue producers were liable to pay. For half a century at least after the conquest of Persia the Arabs had nothing more than the old tax-lists to go upon; in Khurasan and other less accessible Iranian provinces the official ledgers were kept in Persian for half a century longer still, right up to the time, in fact, of Abū Muslim, who was so largely instrumental in hoisting the Abbasids into the saddle.

As relics of that period a number of Persian fiscal and allied financial terms remained in Arabic as part of the vocabulary of the revenue *dīvān,* itself a word reputed to be of Persian extraction. For centuries Iranians continued to bear a reputation for skill in money matters and provided even European tongues with banking terminology, an instance commonly given being the word "cheque."

More than one of the Omayyad caliphs (who prided themselves on their Arabism) was called upon to defend the employment of these "foreign" instruments, trebly unpopular by reason of their nationality, their office, and their over-efficiency, for they were accused of exacting the uttermost farthing—"remembering even the husks of the rice." One Omayyad governor of Basra, compelled to leave the city in haste when its inhabitants broke out in revolt, justified his retention of the *dihqāns* on the grounds that there was a falling off in the revenue when Arabs were employed and that the Persians had a keener eye for what was taxable, were more trustworthy and less extortionate.

The Persian revenue system, as it existed under the first Chosroes, Anūsharvān the Just, was a simple one. All cultivators of the soil paid a percentage of their crops in kind or cash and all full-grown males paid a poll-tax, from which were exempted members of the recognized noble families, great landlords, knights, "scribes," and the king's servants. By and large this was the system perpetuated by 'Umar, with the difference that under his regime the privileged class consisted of the Arabs.

Where the revenue contribution was in cash, payment was made in dirhams, silver coins that under the Sassanians had borne on the obverse the image of the king and on the reverse the picture of a Zoroastrian fire-altar with a ministering priest on either side. In spite of Islamic disapproval of such imagery, these coins were adopted by the Arab invaders, who employed native Persian craftsmen to make what they could. As the old coins became scarcer, Omayyad and Abbasid governors in the eastern provinces had fresh ones struck, of identical type but with the addition of either Pahlavi or Arabic inscriptions, or both. The same type, with altar and priests conventionalized as three parallel lines, was perpetuated in the coinage of the Muslim states of North Africa and even in Moorish Spain, while the weight of the purely Muhammadan silver dirham coined by the reforming Omayyad 'Abd al-Malik for use throughout the caliphate was that of its Persian forerunner. This silver dirham continued to be the standard of currency in the eastern provinces until well on in the fourth/tenth century and for almost as long in Iraq too.

Land-tax (*kharāj*) was from its nature payable when the wheat and barley were gathered in. Anciently, harvest celebrations had coincided with the first day (*Nau-rūz,* "New Day") of the Iranian solar year, which then began at the midsummer solstice, June 21. When, during the Achaemenid period, the date of *Nau-rūz* was advanced to the Spring equinox, March 21, both dates were celebrated in the empire, the newer one being retained in Persia and the original one in Egypt and some of the western provinces as a holiday, but also as the date for payment of *kharāj*. Historians at various times record not only the Sassanian practice, which persisted into Muslim times, of exchanging gifts at *Nau-rūz,* but also the rough horseplay which then took place in the city streets of Iraq and Egypt. During these summer saturnalia no respectably dressed person could venture into the streets without risking his dignity. By the Copts *Nay-rūz* is still retained as New Year's Day, which, owing to vagaries of the almanac, now falls on September 10 or 11.

Under the Omayyads, the Arab aristocracy had replaced the Persian in the social scheme of the caliphate, but a change occurred when that dynasty in its turn was replaced by the Abbasids. By their transfer of the capital of the caliphate from Damascus in Syria to Baghdad in Iraq they proclaimed their intention of being princes of all the faithful, and not of the Arab Muslims alone, and of treating non-Arabs with the consideration which had until then been the prerogative of Arabs alone. That this in practice meant a special measure of privilege for Persians is understandable from the fact that the new caliphs themselves had Persian blood in their veins. In defining Persia they drew its boundaries generously, including within them Turkish-speaking tribes from beyond the Oxus as well as men of Arab stock who had settled in Khurasan during and after the Muslim invasion. In this they were adhering to the popular view, defined in the eleventh century by the constitutional lawyer Māwardī, that whereas the bond between Arabs was intimate blood-kinship, amongst non-Arabs it was geographical propinquity or racial interest.

Naturally enough in view of their origins the Abbasids regarded their empire as a continuation of the Sassanian and their own place in it as exactly corresponding to that of their predecessors. The chief difference was to be that Islam was to replace Zoroastrianism as the state religion, of which they were to be the heads precisely as the Iranian Kings had been. In contrast with the Omayyads, whom the annalists of the Abbasid period depict as irreligious, worldly materialists, the Baghdad caliph was proclaimed a zealous "Protector of the Faithful" and the guardian of orthodoxy. No Abbasid allowed it to be forgotten that he was a kinsman of the Prophet, whose mantle had been transmitted to him. The laws of Islam were moulded to the requirements of the state, and the association of faith and secular sovereignty was placed upon the pedestal which it had occupied in Sassanian Iran and is so constantly praised by Firdausī in his *Shāh-nāma.*

An abiding instance of this close linking of religious with secular functions lies in the conception of the *qāḍī,* primarily a man learned in the Qur'ān and the Traditions, but one whose function was to preside over the courts of law even where they were concerned with civil causes. The parallel with the priest, who dispensed justice under Zoroastrianism, is a fairly clear one.

There were amongst the Sassanians those who on their coins had designated themselves as *bāghī* ("godlike"). The claim to divine honors was also made by, or acceded to, some of the Abbasids, who attempted to create about themselves "that reverential awe," in Gibbon's words, "which distance only, and mystery, can preserve towards an imaginary power." Like the Sassanians they achieved it by secluding themselves from the common gaze, employing as well as curtains and other paraphernalia numerous guards and chamberlains to impede that access to their chiefs which Arabs claimed as a right. The most terrifying of these adjuncts of sovereignty was the personal bodyguard, which always included one or more individuals whose task was immediately and without question to carry out the monarch's commands, however grim. No one who has read the *Arabian Nights* can forget the sinister figure of Masrūr, the slave without whom 'Haroun al-Raschid' never appeared in public. He was, it may here be remarked, a Turkoman of Farghana and not, as is often said, a Negro.

The executioner was the symbol of the absolute power which the Iranian Shāhanshāh wielded over the lives of his subjects and which the Abbasids in their turn arrogated to themselves. It was a pretension which was recognized in public, at any rate, and in the vicinity of the court, but that other views were held privately is a point which emerges from a conversation reported by the annalist Ṭabarī. The caliph Manṣūr had sent one of his freedmen, whom he specially retained for such tasks, to assassinate a man called Fuḍail, groundlessly accused by him of having behaved improperly towards the young prince Ja'far. Hearing of the murder, and unaware of his father's part in it, Ja'far remarked to a companion, "What will the Commander of the Faithful say to the slaying of an innocent Muslim?" The reply was: "He is the Commander of the Faithful. He does what he pleases and knows best what he is about." "You miserable oaf," Ja'far retorted (the Arabic is stronger), "I speak to you in confidence and you give me a public [i.e., a formal and official] answer." Of Manṣūr certainly it is true that he was very conscious of his rights and dignities. Admonishing his son and successor, Mahdī, he said: "Shed no blood unlawfully; it is a sin in God's sight. But defend your sovereignty and destroy anyone who disregards it or dares to withdraw himself from it."

For the administration of the secular affairs of the caliphate Manṣūr is reported to have said that he required four men of integrity: a *qāḍī* at whom no one could point the finger of blame, a police officer who would enforce the claims of the weak against the strong, a tax-gatherer who would press his claims without extortion, and an "intelligence" officer who would submit honest reports on the other three. These officials, leaving aside their qualifications, corresponded to some who formed part of the civil service of the Persian kings. Of the first three something has already been said above. With regard to the fourth, the "intelligence" or "postal (*barīd*) service was taken over from the state postal organizations of

Byzantium and Iran, which provided relays of fast messengers bringing to the capital reports of happenings in the provinces and returning with orders or an occasional visitor of importance. The terminology of the *barīd* system, with some linguistic modifications, enriched the Arabic vocabulary with the Persian words for "courier," "foot messenger," "guide," "post horse," "waybill," and the like. Early in the Abbasid period, too, a whole series of route books was written in Arabic to guide officials of the service; they are of interest now as providing information about geographical and economic conditions in the districts bordering the various roads and in the settlements through which they passed.

A state official not mentioned above, although he was the caliph's right-hand man in the direction of the central government, was the vizier. It is a matter of debate whether he was identical in function with the official of the Sassanian government whom the Persian literature of the Muhammadan period calls vizier. That literature makes constant reference to the great Buzurgmihr, vizier to Anūsharvān the Just, and a character so admirable that he may without hazard be regarded as a personification of the virtues rather than a creature of flesh and blood. Whether he is fictitious or not, it is a fact that the aura of godhead with which the Persian kings surrounded themselves created the need for an intermediary between themselves and the outer world. In earlier times he was the *vazurg-framadhār,* the "great executive" carrying out the king's command, a versatile official able to direct any of the departments of state whether civil or military. Under the later Sassanians he appears to have been replaced by a *dabīrpat* or "chief scribe."

It was a "scribe" also, parallel in function with the Chancellor of medieval European courts, who executed the policy of the Omayyads in their civil administration. The Abbasids replaced him by the vizier (Arabic *wazīr*), whose name, almost certainly Persian in origin, appears with the meaning of "assistant" in a Qur'ānic passage in which Moses asks for Aaron as his *wazīr,* in fact Polonius' "assistant for a state." Similarly the young Hārūn, not yet caliph and "al-Rashīd", is given Yaḥyā ibn Khālid al-Barmakī (the Barmecide) as his *kātib* ("secretary") and vizier. In this post Yaḥyā appears to have had only civil functions, although he was one of the warriors to whose efforts the Abbasids owed their throne.

The Barmakī dynasty of viziers founded by Yaḥyā had originated in Balkh (Bactria), where they were hereditary high priests of the Buddhist[1] temple of Nau Bahār. But though they were not Zoroastrians their sympathies and traditions were Iranian, to judge from their attitude towards their fellow countrymen and their care in celebrating the national festivals. To them is credited the invention or development of a number of *dīvāns,* or government departments, which controlled the central administration at Baghdad for a hundred and fifty years after their own fall from power. Their organization only disappeared, indeed, when the power of the caliphs had reached vanishing-point and the Commander of the Faithful was the mouthpiece of the Buyid robber barons, who, coming from the region of the Caspian Sea, traced their ancestry back to Adam in a direct line through the ancient kings of Persia.

The Abbasid caliphate had by that time reached the nadir of its fortunes, but for long before it had been in the grip of the Turkoman guards whom successive Commanders of the Faithful had paid—one can hardly say employed—for protection. These Turkomans were slaves whom the caliph Mu'taṣim had in the first instance bought in Persia to be his bodyguard. Very soon his successors had to submit to blackmail from their guardians, whose kinsmen were constantly being freshly recruited and had come to form an important constituent of the standing army now being maintained by the state. The rough tribesmen on their way down from their homeland in Central Asia had spent some time in Iranian territory and had been sufficiently influenced by Persian military tradition to acquire its methods and its terminology. They now wore the short Persian tunic (*qabā*), had the Persian mace among their weapons, and carried their arrows in a Persian quiver (of which the name, *tarkash,* may have supplied the French *carquois*). Officers and men drew *jāmakīyāt* ("clothing-allowance": Persian *jāma,* "clothing"), which came to them from the *Dīwān al-Shākirīya* ("office of the slaves": Persian *chākir,* "slave") set up at Baghdad to deal with their organization.

The maintenance of standing slave-armies was continued by the Fatimid and other princes who broke away from the Abbasid

[1] It is not improbable that the Buddhist rosary came to the Arabs by way of Persia and was received by Europe from them.

caliphate, and from amongst them from time to time vigorous individuals arose to become masters of the states they had served. An outstanding personage of this type, one who affected the course of Muslim history, was Aḥmad ibn Ṭūlūn, who, having been sent to be the Abbasid governor of Egypt, made himself independent ruler of that country and Syria and founded the Ṭūlūnid dynasty.

In its most elaborate and complete form the slave state was to be seen in the Mamluk Sultanate of Egypt and Syria, where the rulers, themselves born as slaves, kept a firm control over their subjects by means of large bodies of slaves trained as fighters and a disciplined civil service. It was a system which contained many features originally Persian, notably the *barīd,* and many of the officers of state bore Persian titles. At home in their capital the Mamluks followed the Persian tradition—transmitted through the Fatimids and Abbasids—of maintaining a great display of luxury and ceremonious etiquette. Adoration of royalty was insisted upon so that, when the Sultan appeared, all present bowed down in the attitude usual otherwise only in worship.

The royal household was elaborately organized in departments which, like the officers who had charge of them, bore Persian titles, presumably derived by the Fatimids from those which had at one time been customary at the Iranian court. Many of the officials, more especially those in personal attendance on the Sultan, bore symbols of their functions. The *dawādār* ("scribe") carried a pen box, the Squire a bow, the Master of the Robes a "hold-all," the Marshal a horseshoe, the Taster a round disk representing a table, and the Polo Master a polo stick. Such concrete objects were in course of time replaced by conventionalized representations or blazons, which, imported into Europe by returning crusaders, formed the beginnings of modern heraldry. Of more immediate interest here is the fact that the symbols and the Mamluk officials who bore them were called by Persian names and that the Arabic *rank* ("blazon"), which is derived from the Persian *rang* ("color"), may possibly be the ancestor of our own "rank" and of regimental and other "colors."

There is mention of especially elaborate ceremonial when those Sultans who were addicted to the Persian game of polo went to play. Baibars, for example, the Sultan whose troops stemmed the flood of Mongol invasion and prevented its reaching Egypt, had the custom of playing three games every Saturday in the season after the Nile floods. He would set out at dawn from the royal stables and followed by a cavalcade in festive dress would pass through cheering crowds to the ground constructed by one of Saladin's successors in the neighborhood of the present-day Bab al-Luq at Cairo. He was not, however, at such times accompanied by the royal sunshade—the *chatr,* which was reserved for more solemn occasions.

So far we have been dealing with princes and other important dignitaries, at whose level international contacts had always been possible, whether in peace or war. Long before the Muhammadan conquests Arabs and Persians of all grades of society had in some measure become acquainted, if only through each other's merchandise. From time immemorial traders had brought the products of countries near and far to Arabia, which anciently had busy international markets, or to contiguous ports such as Basra on the Persian Gulf. In return, caravans went annually from central Arabia to Iran and other countries bearing resins for incense, those "perfumes of Arabia" which would not sweeten the hand of Lady Macbeth, linen stuffs, and other luxuries. Abū Sufyān, a fellow tribesman of Muhammad's who bitterly opposed his early claims to prophethood and public recognition, made a fortune for himself and the chiefs of the Quraish tribe by supplying capital for trading ventures into Persia.

Two centuries or more before the emergence of the Prophet there had been a well-known market at Hira, the capital of an Arab kingdom established by the Lakhmī dynasty along the Euphrates, not far from the ancient Babylon. There the Arab kings, for long the vassals of the Sassanian Shāhanshāhs, reproduced the life of the Persian courts and gave traders, pilgrims, poets, and other travelers ideas which they carried back with them to the cities of the Arabian peninsula and elsewhere. They also took back with them articles of Persian make which took their fancy and the native names of which are to be found embedded in even the earliest Arabic literature.

With the coming of Islam contacts became more numerous and intimate. By far the greatest number of the peninsula's inhabitants were nomads, loosely organized in tribes whose members had enjoyed a good measure of liberty both as regards their duties to the commonwealth and to the deities they chose to worship. Their physical requirements were little more than those indispensable to existence and their chief excitement lay in the prosecution of inherited feuds. When, possessed and revitalized by Islam, they burst through the weakened barriers surrounding the empires of Persia and Byzantium, they found themselves amongst peoples long accustomed to the forms of settled existence, with refinements, conventions and amenities which struck them as in many ways desirable.

Like other "empire builders" the advancing Arabs were receptive of the ideas of their new subjects, whose material equipment and ways of life many of them were eager to adopt. The members of the shaikhly families in particular, with their opportunities for penetrating into the households of wealthy Persians, were quick to seize upon the luxuries they found. Within a comparatively few years of the invasion young men attached to the court of the Omayyad caliph were discarding their homespun in favor of expensive clothes of brocaded silk cut in the Persian style, eating Persian culinary delicacies, and displaying Persian manners at tables that were themselves an importation from Persia.

Those of the original invading forces who penetrated as far east as Khurasan settled down amongst the local inhabitants and, quickly imitating them, adopted trousers instead of skirted garments, took to drinking wine, and celebrated the Persian holidays. This did not prevent their continuing their associations with the camp-cities of Iraq from which they had sprung, so that it became a common occurrence to hear Persian spoken in the bazaars of Kufa and Basra. By the time of the early battles of the Abbasids the Khurasani Arab troops spoke as much Persian as Arabic.

With the foundation of Baghdad the caliph Manṣūr intended to bring the east and west of his empire closer together. He was determined, moreover, to endow his capital with the amenities of a great city, and although we cannot tell to what extent the humbler citizens enjoyed them, we have evidence that even fairly unimportant government officials regarded the new importations as necessities. Ṭabarī thinks it worthy of comment that a provincial civil servant peremptorily summoned by the caliph and brought by the *barīd,* i.e., post-haste, had in his luggage a Persian prayer rug, a mattress and cushions, water pot and basin, and, last refinement of all, a copper lye-holder betraying its Persian origin by its name. Manṣūr would probably not have approved such luxury in a subordinate had it been brought to his notice. He had a reputation for niggardliness and once had a secretary thrashed in his presence for wearing trousers made of a material which he regarded as too expensive. He extended his economies to his own person and adhered strictly to the sumptuary laws of Islam, of which he was the head. When the famous Christian physician Bukht-Yishū', on a visit to the palace from the college at Jundi-Shapur in southwest Persia, asked for wine with his dinner, he was told that it was not served at the caliph's table. Whereupon he drank Tigris water, tactfully declaring afterwards that he preferred it.

On the temporal side Manṣūr followed the Sassanian tradition. He insisted that members of his household and his court should never appear in public without being dressed in the most costly embroidered silks and scented with the finest perfumes. His new buildings were of Persian design, and it is evident from the architectural terms employed in Arabic that it was by Persian builders that such features were introduced as arches and domes, porticoes and balustrades, windows, ventilators, and waterspouts. To the outside amenities of large houses they added, after the fashion of their own country, gardens, kiosks (garden pavilions), and fountains. Inside the houses, such furnishings as tables, chairs, mattresses, cushions, and mosquito curtains, a well as the materials for hangings and floor coverings, were further importations from Iran. The kitchen, too, was not neglected. Ovens, frying pans, trays and bowls, mortars and pestles were brought in, to say nothing of the recipes for savory dishes which had been the secrets of Persian housewives and now found their way into Arabic cookbooks.

Wares of this kind, finding their way on to the markets, created a popular demand and stimulated local craftsmen to emulative production. In that way the spinning, weaving, dyeing, and metalworking trades, as well as the decorative arts, with all the chemistry and metallurgy they demanded, received immediate encouragement. Persian designs became common in the products of Arab looms and workshops. Many of the raw materials required were no doubt produced locally, but soft-iron and steel, with certain kinds of bronze, were brought from Iran. So also were the beautiful lapis lazuli and turquoise which gave their rich color to the enamels and glazed ware of the Middle East. One such import worth further mention is amber. Its Persian name, *kahrubā* ("straw-attracter"), became embedded in modern Egyptian Arabic, in which both electricity and the electric tram are designated by it.

Local drugs and medicines also received large additions from Persia, for though in the Arabic medical textbooks many of the anatomical terms are of Greek or Latin origin, in the pharmacology the names most common are Persian. This is not altogether surprising when taken with the fact that for over four centuries one of the most important schools of medicine in the Middle East existed at Jundi-Shapur in Khuzistan, the province whose capital is Ahwaz. The family of Bukht-Yishū', the Christian physician already mentioned, was settled here and for six generations continued to uphold the school's reputation. The tradition of Persian medicine did not end with them, for amongst the Persians who contributed to the fame of "Arab" science in medieval Europe were Rhazes (i.e., the "Man of Ray"), Haly Abbas ('Alī ibn 'Abbās, "The Magian"), and Avicenna of Hamadan.

Perhaps the most important single commodity received by the Arabs through the medium of Iran was rag paper. It was, of course, a Chinese invention, the introduction of which into Persia came about in A.D. 751, when Muslim forces, after a brush with Chinese troops, captured one or two who were paper makers by trade. They taught the art to the Persians, who had hitherto used parchment for their documents. In this connection a story is told of the caliph Manṣūr's having ordered his storekeepers to sell their large stock of Egyptian paper, declaring that henceforth he would follow the Persian example and use nothing but materials produced at home.

Allied with the making of books was the art of binding, which had been greatly improved by Persian methods of tanning that increased the suppleness of leather and made tooling and ornamentation easier. We hear of specially treasured works that were written in gold ink on Chinese paper and had covers of fine leather lined with brocade and adorned with precious stones and gold.

As imported luxuries and "foreign" manners became commoner,

while simultaneously an orthodox form of Islam took concrete shape, the less well-endowed members of the population, who were in general also those who clung most closely to their Arab nationalism and their religion, were inclined to resent them and demand a return to the early ascetic standards. Their feelings are reflected in the sermons of the religious leaders of the age and the admonitions of its moralists, from which a good deal of social history can be gleaned. The religious textbooks of Islam are almost unanimous in their denunciation of music and games, because, it may be inferred, they distracted people from more serious pursuits. The persons chiefly blamed for having introduced them into Arab cities are men of Iranian nationality, and it is a fact that those mentioned in connection with music were people who had come in pursuit of trade, as craftsmen in other arts, or simply as professional musicians.

When 'Abd Allāh ibn Zubair, a rival of the Omayyads for the caliphate, decided that the Ka'ba at Mecca needed repair, he hired Persian and Greek masons to do the work. Like other craftsmen they sang as they worked, and their tunes appear to have taken the fancy of the local inhabitants. What songs the Grecians sang is lost to memory, but there is frequent reference in Arabic literature to the music of the Persians, some of whom had brought instruments with them which they taught the Meccans to play. Not content with playing, the Meccans and other Arabs learned how to construct instruments of their own and establish their own system. Yet as late as the year 300 of the Hijra (A.D. 912) the Baghdad inventor of a new instrument gave it a Persian name.

Under the Omayyads, members of the richer families were eager patrons of music and dancing, going to the extent of bringing to Damascus and other cities in their domains directly from Persia performers in both arts and of both sexes. Their enthusiasm did not fade when, displaced by the Abbasids and driven from Syria, they set up a monarchy in Andalusia. At the court of the second 'Abd al-Raḥmān of Cordova (A.D. 822-52) a Persian singer named Zaryāb ("Gold-finder"), who had at one time been a client of the Abbasid caliph Mahdī, made his mark so effectively that he became a "star," whose clothes and mannerisms set the fashion and whose taste, even in the art of cookery, was declared to be impeccable.

In the eastern caliphate the demand for Persian music was such that many an impresario made a large fortune out of it. The Arabic anthology *Kitāb al-Aghānī* ("Book of Songs"), the compilation of Abu 'l-Faraj of Isfahan, makes constant reference to the huge fees paid to, or expected by, successful singers and players. It tells also of an entrepreneur—whose father, incidentally, bore the Persian nickname of *Bisyār-diram* ("Many pence")—who spent a large sum of money in adding an extension to his house for public performances.

Among pastimes other than music regularly claimed by Arabic writers to have been introduced from Persia are the games of polo, chess, and *nard* (*trictrac* or backgammon). Hārūn al-Rashīd is declared to have been the first caliph to play polo, but long before his time the game had formed part of the Persian nobleman's education. The essayist Ibn Qutaiba cites an old Persian manual on royal deportment that includes a section devoted to the rules and etiquette of the game and hints on play. The learner is instructed how to handle the mallet and control his pony, and careful attention is paid to the manners desirable on the field. Thus the player may not apply his whip to the ball if he has missed with his mallet, which should never be allowed to dig up the ground or injure the pony's legs; care must be taken to avoid disabling other players, of either side, by collision or otherwise; there must be no display of bad temper, nor any cursing or swearing, and balls should not be recklessly driven out of the field "even if they are six a penny." Spectators, finally, should not be excluded but should be allowed to sit on the enclosing wall of the *maidān* (ground), the width of which was fixed at sixty cubits especially to include them.

Mention has already been made of Sultan Baibars' devotion to the game. A more famous addict was Saladin, while amongst fictional characters who played was King Yūnān of the *Arabian Nights* who, on the advice of the sage Dūbān, played "hockey on horseback" (Burton) and so was cured of his maladies by the medicine contained in the handle of the "goff-stick" (Lane).

As for chess, whatever its origins may have been, its passage through Persia left it in the form which the Arabs inherited together with some of the Persian terminology. *Shaṭranj* remained the name for chess (i.e., *Shāh,* German *Schach*) and *shāh* for the king, with *shāh-māt* as "checkmate." The queen was still the "counsellor" (*firzān* or *farzīn;* cf. Old French *vierge*), the bishop the "elephant" (*fīl;* cf. French *fou*), and the "castle" or "chariot," *rukh*. In the more popular game of *nard,* the French name of which, *trictrac,* appears to represent the click of the dice on the board, the Persian numbers were long retained for scoring, as the *Kitāb al-Aghānī* shows in more than one anecdote.

A common and absorbing pastime in a society where books were rare and literacy unusual was that of listening to stories. By the learned, who form the religious opinion of Islam, romances and works of fiction have always, like music, been condemned as unworthy of the attention of serious men—and gravity is a prime virtue amongst Arabs. Nevertheless, the storyteller's art has always been a highly valued accomplishment and new material eagerly sought for. The audience of even Muḥammad the Prophet dwindled away to join that of his rival, Naḍr ibn al-Ḥārith, who was narrating the Persian legend of Rustam and Isfandiyār. Naḍr's comment when he heard of the Prophet's anger was, "By Allah, Muhammad cannot tell a better tale than mine." In their intercourse for trade and on other occasions Persian and Arab travelers exchanged news, ideas, and anecdotes, the Persian contribution towards the latter probably being very considerable. It cannot be claimed that all the romances of the *Arabian Nights* were importations, but the "framework" story, with its Persian characters Shahryār, Sheherāzād, and the rest, together with some in the body of the collection, bear unmistakable marks of their Iranian provenance. To go farther into that question here would be to trespass on the ground of the Persians' contribution to Arabic literature.

There remains to be said something about the impact of Iranian thought and feeling on Arab collective life. In recent times the theory has been propounded that the conquering Arabs' religion was genuinely embraced only by the nobles and the wealthy among the subdued people of Iran, and then only as a security measure. The masses, it is held, clung to their old beliefs, paying lip service to the new creed, which they cast off as soon as they felt strong enough in combination to do so. For such renegation they would never have lacked leaders, Persia having throughout the centuries been prolific in men claiming to possess divine inspiration that demanded mankind's attention. For illustration there need only be recalled the names of Mani and the Manichaeans, Mazdak (the dualist "reformer" of Zoroastrianism), Bābak the Khurramite, al-Muqanna' (the "veiled" prophet) of Khurasan, and 'Abd Allāh ibn Maimūn al-Qaddāḥ (the alleged founder of the Ismā'īlī sect) among older claimants, and the "Bāb" amongst the modern ones.

Whether the theory can be proved awaits further investigation. In the meantime, evidence of the persistence of Iranian beliefs and their spread even among native Arab communities is to be found in the heresy-hunting by religious authorities almost before the time when a conception of orthodoxy had been formulated. *Zindīqs,* as heretics were called—the name is Iranian—were to be found in any of the social strata, one report including even the caliph Ma'mūn himself. The character of the charge leveled against them was not constant. Under the Omayyads it was not so much religious as political, it being held that as they were not completely reconciled to Islam they were hostile to the caliph at its head and hence to the Muslim state. Under the Abbasids, who laid more stress than their predecessors on the religious side of their office, the test was dogma. By strict inquiry into beliefs they checked any possibility of political revolt amongst those Persians whose promotion to eminent positions in the state might have encouraged a revival of national sentiment.

A regular inquisitorial system was inaugurated soon after the accession of the Abbasids to power. The caliph Mahdī appointed special officers to direct it, and in his last testament urged his son and successor to destroy dualists, the advocates of Iranianism. The inclusion of Ma'mūn among the *zindīqs* can have had no other foundation than his liberalism and the tolerance he showed towards those whom pious Muslims regarded as lax. A remark made by a Zoroastrian whom the caliph had advised to turn Muhammadan sheds light on this point. "Your advice is good," said the man, "but you are not among those who would compel men to renounce their [own] faith."

Under Ma'mūn the cult of Iranianism appears to have been something of a pose. A certain Ibn Ziyād, a member of the Baghdad intelligentsia accused of being a *zindīq,* had the following squib thrown at him by a poet friend:

O son of Ziyād, O Ja'far's father,
No heretic are you but rather

A Musulman true in faith and fact,
Tho' like a heretic you act:
Sole aim and goal of your endeavour—
To show the world that you are clever.

That Persians did, however, cling to the faith of their fathers in predominantly Muslim surroundings was made clear during the trial for heresy of the distinguished Persian general Afshīn. He had been employed by the caliph Mu'taṣim to destroy the heretic Bābak the Khurramite, and had succeeded. But he had incurred the jealousy and enmity of rivals, who aimed to bring him low on a charge of heresy on his own part. In spite of his services to the caliph, he was arrested and brought to trial. The first witnesses to confront him were the muezzin and imām of a mosque who accused him of having had them beaten until their bones were stripped of flesh. His defense was that these two men, in spite of an agreement made with the local ruler—a Soghdian—that his subjects would be allowed to worship as they pleased, had attacked the local temple, thrown out its idols, and converted the building into a mosque.

Afshīn was then asked to account for his possession of a heretical work so elaborately ornamented with gold, jewels, and brocade that it must have a special value for him. He replied that it was an heirloom, that it contained material devoted to Persian ethics, which he practiced, and that he disregarded anything else in it. As for the ornamentation, it was on the book when he had received it and he had never seen any more reason to remove it than the caliph himself from his copy of the *Kalīla wa-Dimna,* the famous book of Indian fables.

A Zoroastrian priest lately converted to Islam was next called. His evidence was that Afshīn had induced him to eat the flesh of animals not slaughtered according to the Muslim rites, but, graver still, that Afshīn had admitted he had put himself among "these people" and done all that he detested, yet had never been circumcised. Afshīn turned on the man for having betrayed his confidences and asked, "Did I not of my own accord admit you to my house and acknowledge that I favored Persianism and those who believed in it?"

He was then confronted by a border chieftain who declared that Afshīn's people, when writing to him, addressed him as "God of gods." That, said Afshīn, was a traditional title which he preserved only for the sake of his prestige with his tribe. When the question of his circumcision was put to him again he protested: "Surely, *taqīya* (concealment of one's beliefs where an avowal of them would be hazardous) is an admitted practice in Islam? I feared that circumcision would endanger my life." This protest was swept away with the retort that he had never hesitated to fling himself against spear and sword on the battlefield, and in the end he was found guilty and put to death.

The admissions of a man of Afshīn's status would appear to invalidate the theory that it was only the poorer class of Persians who were loyal to their old faith. It is true that some among the new Muslims were too poor to carry out all the duties required of them, that some were lax and some skeptical enough to write epigrams saying that the rich had motives for cultivating Allāh that were not given to the impecunious. It is equally true that many of the poor were strict in their observances, even to the extent of performing the pilgrimage to Mecca, from which the law absolved them.

However, that may be, revolts against established authority from time to time broke out in Persia and spread to Arab lands, where they found considerable support. According to the famous vizier, Niẓām al-Mulk, who is associated in story with 'Umar Khaiyām and Ḥasan-i Ṣabbāḥ ("Grand Master of the Assassins"), the Ismā'īlī movement was started by a native of Ahwaz, a certain 'Abd Allāh ibn Maimūn al-Qaddāḥ. Its basic principle is that of official Shī'ism, namely, the divine right of the Prophet's descendants to be Commanders of the Faithful, as opposed to the Sunnī claim, which is that caliphs must be elected. Both Ismā'īlism and its parent, Shī'ism, believed that the last Imām ("Leader" of the faith) and the Prophet's last earthly successor would be the Mahdī, the harbinger of the restoration of the kingdom of righteousness on earth. Where they differed was over the number of Imāms to be reckoned between him and the caliph 'Alī, the first of them.

With amazing speed the movement covered the Muslim world. To quote the Niẓām al-Mulk again: "These accursed people emerged in Syria, the Yemen and Andalusia, and if a full statement of their activities is required, recourse must be had to the histories, especially that of Isfahan." The arguments they used to secure converts differed with the persons they had as their objective, and the names by which they designated themselves varied with time and place. In Egypt and Aleppo they were *Ismā'īlīs,* in Transoxiana and Ghazna *Qarmaṭīs,* in Kufa *Mubārakīs,* in Ray (Rhages) *Bāṭinīs,* and so forth. But all," says our author, "have one object in common—the overthrow of Islam."

For the Arab world the political and social consequences of Ismā'īlism were many and far-reaching. It gained adherents by the method, not unknown to modern politics, of sending missionaries to form "cells" of converts. These were admitted only after a careful preliminary initiation, and since the propagandists had to deal with all sorts and conditions of men they had to be prepared for argument and discussion. Out of this necessity grew considerable intellectual stimulation and an eagerness to acquire the learning and philosophies of the time.

For this matter to be viewed in its proper perspective, something must first be said of the political development of Ismā'īlism amongst the Arab communities. Towards the end of the third century of the Hijra (about the beginning of the tenth century A.D.), the grandson of that 'Abd Allāh ibn Maimūn al-Qaddāḥ already mentioned as the founder of Ismā'īlism appeared under the name of 'Ubaid Allāh among the Berbers of North Africa with the claim that he was a descendant of Fāṭima, the Prophet's daughter. The way had been prepared for him by propagandists using Ismā'īlī methods and doctrines as a screen for the political ambitions of their leader, who now proclaimed himself to be the Mahdī. Within a relatively short time he made himself master of the Maghrib and became the first caliph of the Fatimid dynasty. The fourth of that line put the family in possession of Egypt, which remained in their hands until Saladin deprived them of it.

The sixth Fatimid, who reigned over Egypt and Syria under the title of al-Ḥākim, was a strange character who could be murderously cruel and at the same time a generous patron of the arts. He is usually described as insane by the Muslim historians, but he applied method to his pursuit of power. When he was proclaimed by two Persian Ismā'īlīs to be the incarnation of God on earth he encouraged the idea, which naturally caused offense to the more piously minded Cairenes. One of the two propagandists, a man named Darazī, fled to Syria, where he continued his mission among a section of the inhabitants of the Lebanon and Palestine who are known after him as the "Druzes" and continued to believe in the divinity of al-Ḥākim.

The Persian genius for intrigue and the secret diffusion of occult doctrine was displayed in its most dramatic form by that sect of the Ismā'īlīs which achieved notoriety in the annals of the crusades under the name of Assassins. Like war to modern statesmen, murder was to them an extension of political argument, but it was not the only or even the chief means of persuasion they used. Indeed, to regard the Ismā'īlī Assassins just as brutal and bloodthirsty "gangsters" is to misunderstand their motive, which was, in a politically unsettled world, to introduce what they regarded as the stable system of the Imāmate with its principle of established authority.

The founder of the sect was Ḥasan-i Ṣabbāḥ, an emissary of the Fatimids and a native of Persia, to which country his father had emigrated from the Yemen. His "New Propaganda" seems to have been designed to divert the loyalty of Ismā'īlīs from the older leaders to himself. In A.D. 1090 he got possession of the rock fortress of Alamut, near Qazvin, and from there he carried on his secret campaign until he had built up solidly organized bodies of adherents in Persia, Mesopotamia, and Syria. It was at this time that the rivalry of the Seljuk Sultans (who were strict Sunnīs) with the Fatimid caliphs of Egypt made the crusades possible, and the "Old Man of the Mountains," who created such terror among the European warriors, was the chief of the Syrian Ismā'īlīs. Now, as has been indicated, Ismā'īlism was a cultural as well as a political movement. One year after the Fatimid conquest of Egypt came the foundation of the mosque al-Azhar, which developed, as the need grew to equip emissaries with learning, into the university *par excellence* of Islam. It has changed its character in the course of its history, but in Fatimid days, when it became established as a place of learning, there was close connection between the exponents of Fatimid doctrines and the philosophers of the Ismā'īlī movement, many of whom were Persians, as, for example, Abū Ya'qūb of Sistan, Abū Ḥātim of Ray, Nāṣir-i Khusrau (the Persian "Faust"), and Ḥasan-i Ṣabbāḥ himself. The historian Juvainī, who accompanied the Mongol forces which stormed Alamut, found large quantities of books in the fortress, as well as astrological and alchemical apparatus.

The intellectual activity which this implies is now reliably connected with the work of the group of encyclopaedists known as "the Brethren of Purity" (*Ikhwān al-Ṣafā*). At the time when the Fatimids were consolidating their dominion in Egypt and the Ismā'īlīs actively propagating their teachings in Khurasan, the encyclopaedists from their center at Basra were elaborating a "secret religion for the enlightened man." They expounded it in a series of Arabic treatises dealing with the concrete and abstract constituents of the universe in a mixture of Greek philosophy, gnosticism, and the dualist conceptions of Iranian religion. These treatises were regarded by the adherents of Ismā'īlism as "glorious" fountains of illumination, a title which indicates the place they held in what orthodox Islam regarded as a gross heresy.

Curiously related to the political organization of the Fatimids, and the Ismā'īlīs generally, was the practice of men following the same trade or craft of grouping themselves about a shaikh or senior who acted as their spokesman and was in some measure answerable for them to the ruling authority. Such groups were not completely identical with the guilds of medieval Europe because of the religious or even mystical element included in the conditions of membership. But we learn that a semi-religious body like the Carmathians, who came to be merged into the Ismā'īlīs, was largely composed of fellahin and craftsmen. The organization of such bodies was greatly elaborated under the Fatimids, in whose time the custom of reserving whole bazaars for particular wares was extended throughout the Muhammadan world.

From their very nature it was inevitable that the guilds should claim Muḥammad the Prophet as their founder. Next to him in the chain of authority came the Imān 'Alī and then the peculiar patron of all guilds, Salmān Pāk the Persian, who was the Prophet's barber. Immediately under him stands the elder (Persian *pīr*) or ancestor of each individual trade group. Salmān Pāk is also regarded as the patron of an order of knighthood (*futuwwa*), of which the most illustrious member was the Abbasid caliph al-Nāṣir (A.D. 1180-1225). Members of the order wore a distinguishing costume, of which the most notable part was a pair of breeches, in general the dress of the Persian, as opposed to the Arab skirt. The drawing on of these garments seems to have been the culmination of the ceremony of induction into the order.

Something of the extent of the membership may be gathered from the journals of the Spanish poet and traveller Ibn Jubair, who, while on a pilgrimage to Mecca, seized the opportunity of visiting some of the cities of Egypt and Syria. He found that at Damascus and other Syrian towns the Sunnīs were outnumbered by the "heretical" Shī'a, who were composed of various sects—Rāfiḍīs, Imāmīs, Zaidīs, Ismā'īlīs, Nuṣairīs ("These are misbelievers who attribute godhead to 'Alī"), and others. Chief among the sects was that of the *Nubūwīya* ("Prophetists"), "Sunnīs who are supporters of the *futuwwa.*" Those who achieved distinction in the order were given the breeches to wear. An early stage in the development of the group is perhaps referred to by the historian, Ibn Qutaiba of Merv (A.D. 885), who, when speaking of chivalrous conduct, quotes a tradition of the caliph 'Umar to the following effect: "Wear loincloth, cloak and sandals [i.e., Arab dress]. Throw away top boots, girth, and stirrups and mount your horse at a bound. Let luxury and Persian costume go and never wear silk."

Still another section of Arab-Muslim society with which the name of Salmān the Persian is connected is that of the dervishes. Though the word *darvīsh* itself has an Iranian origin, it would be going far beyond the limits of this essay to trace the part played by Persia in the history of the movement. It must suffice to indicate the fact that among dervish orders the best known (e.g. the Qādirīs and Mevlevīs) had founders whose connections with Iran were especially close.

4

THE ROLE OF THE TURKS IN ISLAM

Julius Germanus

Central Asia, that desiccated highland of roaming nomads, was probably the original home of a race of peoples whom we generally call *Turks* but who as far as their ethnographic appearance and habits of life go are closely connected with the Mongolians with whom they also have an affinity of language. Their history is older than written documents. Their existence as a factor in the history of Asia far precedes our classification of races in an anthropological or linguistic sense. The Chinese chronicles mention them as early as 1300 B.C., and the role which they played in later centuries was distinctly foreshadowed by those conglomerations of peoples who in the second century B.C. harassed the northern frontier of China. These *Hiung-nu,* probably the Huns of the Middle Ages, and the *Yuen-Yuen,* probably the Avars, and the *Tu-kiu* were warlike tribes uniting under one powerful leader who conducted their marauding expeditions against strangers and relatives alike. National or even racial consciousness did not exist; and in the hordes of these restless spirits of the steppes many non-Turkish elements also fought. The people of the Middle Ages, like the ancients, had no ear for linguistic differences; it was the cult, the habits of life, which attracted their attention and they defined peoples according to their appearances and called them Scythians or Hiung-nu or Turks without any attempt at a linguistic definition. The language of these hordes was

Reprinted, with permission, from *Islamic Culture,* VII (1933), 519-32 and VIII (1934), 1-14. Minor ommissions have been made.

not uniform; Uralian, Iranian, and Mongolian were represented in their ranks, but the form of organization and their primitive creed of fire-worship, Shamanism, and Buddhism, later on Christianity and Islam, changing and mixing with the new admixture of blood and their characteristic nomadic culture, distinguished them from the Iranian settlers, the Chinese rice-cultivators, the Hindus, and the Christian Aryans of Europe. This form of organization, which crystallized around a leader who had undisputed sway over the tribes united under him, which based its economic and State existence on intimidating and subduing peoples settled in fruitful territories and abandoning to them the peaceful pursuits of industry while they restricted themselves to the management of State affairs, we may call *Turanian*. Turanian does not imply a linguistic definition, as many Ural-Altaian and Aryan peoples were comprised within this term, but it implies contradistinction to Iranian, to the settled town-dwelling population, with a distinct cult and theology and social class organization, one ever crystallizing, breaking up, recrystallizing; roaming hordes without culture of their own but with elements of culture from all the peoples with whom they came in contact. The language of the ruling class was in most cases Turkish. It seems very probable that the mother-tongue of Attila and Bayan and even Chengiz Khan was Turkish, and the few remains of written culture such as the golden treasure of Attila in the Vienna Museum bear Turkish inscriptions; moreover the language of the inscriptions of Orkhon and Yenisei is also Turkish.

This type of society, very active and mobile, enabled the Turanian to cover distances from the confines of China as far as Eastern Europe, and its characteristic open-mindedness admitted the impression of all cultures. They carried Nestorian Christianity and Persian fire worship into China; they are responsible for the overland intercourse between China and India; later they transplanted Islam to Europe. They exported Chinese silk to Byzantium, which trade brought them into collision with Persia and into alliance with Byzantium and Abyssinia, at the time when the Prophet was born. It is characteristic that the most ancient Buddhist temple in Japan contains Persian objects which must have been brought across Asia by Turkish caravans.

It was the awe and respect inspired by personality which created the States of the Turanians. They were never nations—as the constituting elements belonged to two continents—but they were ready and subservient to obey a personality who brought them into a camp. The tent of the virile and active personality, a genius in strategy, was the pivot of empires and the Turks understood how to obey and how to command; and in no time the radiation of the personal will brought millions into obedience. It was this personal will which kept the discordant elements of a Turanian State together, and when such a will ceased to act or when another virile personality challenged it, the empires broke down as suddenly as they arose and gave way to new formations on the same basis. The geographic configuration and the spirit of the peoples which resulted from it and its history has produced an imprint on their character too deep to be changed easily. For long centuries every Turanian people has set up the same type of State organization; the rule of the armed camp over an intimidated population, and out of this rule a mixed culture sprang which was called after the founder of the dynasty and not the nation. Turanian nations received their names from great personalities.

To become a personality was the ambition of the Turanian youth. A personality, not in abstract thinking or meditation like the Hindus, or in sacrificing this earthly world for communion with the Absolute, but a personality of warlike activity, to conquer, to rule, to act. And the essence of politics is activity; so the Turks, being born politicians, have created and destroyed more States than any other people of the world. The Seljuks, who from an insignificant family through fortune and valor rose to the sovereignty of three empires, gave the impetus to another Turkish clan, that of the Ghaznevids, to create a realm in India. The knights readily responded to the call of any hero, and while establishing empires in Persia, Syria, Asia Minor, and India, they were so unmindful of their nationality that they imbibed Persian culture and became Persianized in taste. The *Shâh-nâmah* which immortalizes the feats of Persians at the cost of their Turanian foes was written for a Turkish Prince, and the Seljuk monarchs of Asia Minor had its noble lines engraved in their palaces.

It was the merit of the Seljuk Turks to keep up the tottering Abbasid empire against the Crusaders in Syria. They established a kingdom in Asia Minor, which for more than two centuries planted the seeds of Islamic culture. At Konia, the ancient Iconium, a few miles distant from the caves of St. Paul, one of the greatest Persian poets, Jelal ud-din Rumi, lies buried under a cupola of green tiles. The schools and palaces of the Seljuks, in Persian style with an admixture of Byzantine Greek, commemorate their exquisite taste and love of learning and art.

The Byzantine empire, which was the extreme outpost of Christianity towards the East, was convulsed by the discords of sects and impoverished by an unparalleled maladministration. Vexatious exaction of taxes and sensual court life, with a system of favoritism, sapped the vital forces of this once mighty empire, and the long duration of its agony was due rather to the inertia of a system and to the temporary effort of some martial emperors than to its intrinsic power. Its destiny was sealed, its fertile territories with a dissatisfied population readily lent themselves to any conqueror who brought rule and discipline.

The Mongol wave, which started, like so many of its kind, from the frontiers of China, pushed forward as far as the Alps, stirred up the cauldron of Asia, destroying some peoples and dislodging others, and drove small hordes of Turks belonging to the tribe of Kay Khan across the Caucasus into Asia Minor. They sought shelter at the court of the Seljuk 'Ala ud-din Kay Kobad, and he allowed them, as a reward for their services, to settle near Angora. Further services to the Seljuks brought an aggrandizement of their fiefs, which extended toward the West of Asia Minor. The Seljuk empire in Anatolia was near to its fall. The renewed attacks of the Mongols did not rally its vassals to its succor but on the contrary the local chieftains hoped to aggrandize their territory at the cost of the empire. The Turks of the Kay Khan conquered fortresses from the Greeks on the northwestern shores of Asia Minor and by an adroit alliance with some local Christian vassals soon mastered Aynegol, Bilejik, and Yar Hissar. The Kay Khanlis became one of the most important vassals of the tottering Seljuk kingdom.

The Kay Khanlis were Turks like those who had settled in Asia Minor before them; their dialect was only slightly different, but while the Seljuks had been Muslims for centuries, these newcomers still adhered to their primitive creed of nomads. The legend of the marriage of their chief, Ertogrul's son Osmân, permits us to think that Islam was adopted by them, only in Asia Minor where they had come into a Muslim atmosphere. Osmân, who about 1300 declared his independence of the Seljuks and pursued his conquests against the Greeks, established good government throughout his dominions, which at his death in 1326 extended southward to Kutahia, northward to the sea of Marmara and as far as the valleys of the Sakaria and Adranos.

After the collapse of the Seljuks a number of vassals became independent lords, not recognizing the sovereignty of Karaman Oghlu, who considered himself the natural successor of the Seljuks in their possessions. Aydîn, Sarukhân, Menteshe, Kermiân, and the rest installed an independent court in their dominions and a great many Turkoman tribes roamed in the valleys. The house of Osmân, which by his ascendency firmly established itself in the northwest, acquired a geographical superiority over the rest of the rival clans which were militarily much stronger. The Karamans were shut off from the sea, and their expansion into a kingdom was rendered hazardous by the rivals surrounding them while those of Aydîn, Menteshe, and Kermiân were much too near the sea and were exposed to punitive crusades following their raids. The Ottomans or Osmânlis, who like other Turks henceforward called themselves after their brave leader, were posted in the most fertile territories of Anatolia, in the vicinity of the seat of the Byzantine Empire; with easy access to Europe, to those provinces whose exasperated populations were unwilling to make resistance. Osmân and his successors Orkhân and Murâd could easily have been led into the temptation to conquer Asia Minor and to aspire to the inheritance of the Seljuk kingdom. Such a policy would have led to disastrous wars with rivals and, in default of a military base of operation toward the East and South, without a fleet, exposed to the flanking enterprises of the Ægean Turks, would have been the grave of the House of Osmân. The geographical situation, between the sea of Marmara and the highlands of Central Anatolia, pointed toward an encircling movement round the capital, and while the Ottomans were undisturbed by their Eastern rivals they transferred the center of their activity to the Balkans. Very early, already in 1366, they advanced on their marauding expeditions as far as the lower Danube and defeated Louis of Anjou, who escaped with his bare life. Adrianople and Philopopolis had fallen into their hands a few years earlier. Brûsa had been the capital of the young State for forty years only and the center of gravity was soon on the Balkan peninsula, with Adrianople as capital. Europe was alarmed and gathered troops desperately to expel the Ottomans when, their dangerous nature unsuspected, they were still tolerated by their Asiatic rivals. It was only after Muhammad II, the Conqueror, had captured Constantinople in 1453 that he turned his victorious arms against the Anatolian princes.

The wave of victory and conquest remained unchecked. In 1492 the Turks ravaged Syria, and while the last stronghold of Islam fell in Spain, the Turks more than compensated for the loss. While the Moors in Spain lost their attacking force at the battle of Tours, and lingered on in Spanish towns developing and ripening the fruits of Islamic learning, the new enemy of Europe from the East pushed forward to the gates of Vienna, to the Atlantic Ocean and to the northern shores of the Black Sea, while victory over Egypt crowned the head of the Turkish Sultâns with the laurels of Khadim ul-Harameyn. From a small village community, in two centuries, a world-power had arisen which in its extent, wealth of resources and variety of culture equaled any of the great empires of history. Islamic in religion and culture, the Turkish empire breathed the spirit of the central Asiatic steppes. Greek, Kurd, Persian, Arab, Albanian, Slav, Hungarian, and German and a variety of religions were represented among its subjects. The very name of Turks became awe-inspiring and it was thought impossible to defeat or to destroy them. What human efforts failed to attain, time achieved in its course—time which was helped by the intrinsic weakness of the Turanian system of rule and government. The year 1600 is the high water-mark in the ascendency of the Ottoman power. A century later it was deprived of its Hungarian provinces and, from this time on, reverses followed in quick succession, and so uninterruptedly that the cause of the discomfiture cannot be looked for in the incapacity of unfortunate generals or in the higher genius of the adversary, but in an organic disease of the structure of the State, of its society, and of its methods of rule, and of its spirit. On the other hand as we have to deal with a State antagonistic to Europe, we have to search for the causes which first weakened Europe in face of the Ottomans, then for those which brought about its superiority in the eighteenth and nineteenth centuries. Thus the causes were both external and internal.

The Ottomans during their ascendancy had to fight nations from a favorable strategical position, nations whose State machinery was debilitated and who could not oppose the better equipped and enthusiastic Turks with equal forces. Christian Europe was at loggerheads, the little States of the Balkans were jealous neighbors, and when they met the Turks in a united army on the battlefield this jealousy more than once, caused heavy discomfiture. The whole of Europe could not muster 40,000 men of a regular army to oppose the Turks, whose Janissaries soon became the most efficient fighters of Europe. The feudal system of Europe decentralized the States and weakened their power at the cost of haughty nobles, and the States depended for their policy and much more for their strategy on the nobility, who considered warfare a chivalrous game and not a stake of the fortune of nations. The backbone of the Turkish army was the Janissary, an intrepid well-disciplined veteran who, in constant training under strict and brave officers, was a blind tool in the hands of the Sultân. Eclectic as the culture of the Turanians was, their strategy and military genius were equally opportune. The strategy of the central Asiatic steppes was borrowed from the ancient Persians but the Turk, a born soldier, had a sharp eye to notice the changes of the time and to adopt any innovation in strategy which was necessitated by new inventions and new situations. The Turkish army used the most modern weapons of all Europe while the single State which it attacked possessed only a . . . partially up-to-date equipment. They soon found out the importance of artillery and improved the different calibers to such perfection that no fortification could withstand their destructive powers. At the siege of Constantinople bronze guns of 45 cm. caliber were used. The fortifications in Eastern Europe were built against horsemen and light artillery, with perpendicular high walls; but the Turkish heavy artillery soon necessitated a new system of slanting lower ramparts which came into use at the end of the sixteenth century. Besides these technical causes of superiority the Turks were superior in their enthusiastic spirit, elated after every victory, enriched with the spoils of warfare and animated to fight in the path of Allah. Islam and its martial spirit was one of the greatest motives in the uninterrupted success of the Turks. They had fought, as idolators before, for the sake of rapine and glory, but the propagation of the faith gave a moral aim to their valor and enhanced their fighting qualities. The first Sultâns were bred in the simple and healthy atmosphere of the camp, shared the intrepidity of their soldiers, and excelled their contemporaries in military genius.

When the Ottoman power reached its climax in extension of territories it had to face more numerous and stronger enemies than at the outset of its victorious career, when only the decaying Byzantine empire and the Balkans were encountered. Its strategic situation became weaker as it gradually extended from Anatolia and the lines of communication became longer. The seventeenth century created an altered Europe. Discoveries and inventions, the scientific method of research, the termination of the wars of Reformation and the issue of strong national States with a distinct consciousness of their own, ripened a more capable species of Europeans than the feudal Middle Ages with their scanty and ill-digested learning. State alliances prepared the way for campaigns, and European regular armies, with technical superiority and spiritually advanced, proved dangerous and unconquerable foes. The discovery of America, and the vendibility of its products in the seventeenth century, transferred the commerce of the world from the Mediterranean to the Atlantic Ocean. The circumnavigation of Africa and the changes in the routes of world traffic materially impaired the development of Turkey, as it became, so to speak, excluded from the intercourse of progressive nations. Italy also suffered economically from the same reason, but was able to preserve its cultural treasures and even develop them, while in Turkey, with the stoppage of conquest the sources of cultural enrichment from the subdued and highly endowed peoples also came to an end. Turkey became isolated, cut off from the circulation of new ideas; and while these new ideas mightily revived Europe and led her to study on a comparative basis the cultures of the East, Turkey adhered to antiquated systems and decayed institutions. While, since the Reformation, the European spirit shelved superstitious and clerical ideas, Turkey fell a prey to a privileged class, who tried to stifle the spirit of development in Islam.

One of the internal causes which weakened Turkey was that, with the increase of its territory, it was impossible to control the long lines of communication, and in order to secure connections with the frontiers the intermediate territories were granted a kind of semi-autonomy. Such was the case with the Crimea, Wallachia, and Hungary, while Arabia, North Africa, Egypt, Tripoli, and Algiers were semi-independent provinces. The provinces seemed to be loosely attached to the motherland, Asia Minor. The larger the empire the more variegated it became as to nationalities and religions, which had no common ties with the ruling nation. Internal dissensions and revolts began to weaken the body politic.

The greatest and most deeply operative factor in the dismemberment of the Turkish State was the decay of the ruling spirit which was embodied in the personality of the ruler. We have seen above that the Turanian type of State was based entirely on personality, and this type could easily be combined with the religion of Islam, which, though democratic in its spirit, did not prevent autocrats from concentrating in their hands all the executive power of the State. The Caliph, as highest guardian of the Sheriat, and the Sultân, as temporal ruler of the Turks, combined in creating a unique factor in the person of the ruler who practically owned the whole empire and whose slaves (*qul*) the whole population were. We shall observe the organization of the State machinery later; suffice it to say here that with the weakness of the ruler, the whole system began to crumble. The first great Sultâns down to Selîm II, who received the nickname *mest* (drunken), were active warlike sovereigns who held the administration of the country firmly in their hands and conducted military operations in person. Of eight Sultâns after Selîm, five did not accompany a single military enterprise, but became invisible to their people and spent their lives in the harem. The princes were first murdered, out of fear of sedition, later imprisoned for life. When any of them ascended the throne the life they had spent among eunuchs and irresponsible people had totally unmanned them for the serious duties of the State. The Sultâns became puppets in the hands of a demoralized officialdom; bribery, intrigues, and slander began to give direction to the history of the palace; and the external governors, taking advantage of the demoralized state of the center, sought to enrich themselves in any illegal way. The corruption of Byzantium and sensual amusements invaded the magnificent State machinery which had been created by the able hands of the first Sultans, and undermined the foundation of the empire built up by the bloody sacrifices of the Turkish nation. The external expansion of the empire was stopped; a rapid decrease of the territory caused a fearful deficit in the treasury; while luxury was growing amid the reckless and wanton official class. Revolts, discomfiture, and heavy indemnities inflicted an alarming burden on the remaining part of the people, which had to labor under a growing disadvantage. The Janissaries, who were the mainstay of the army and the pledge of victory, associated themselves with Bektashis and other turbulent elements, and became a standing menace to tranquillity till the great reformer, Mahmûd II, had to destroy them. The administration of the empire, even if it had been conducted in an exemplary way, was out of date; but it was impossible to supplant it with an efficient system on account of the resistance of a fanaticized populace and corrupted officialdom.

Organic was the disease which penetrated from above gradually into the lower strata of society, and for long centuries society was subjected to moral strains which no nation could endure with impunity. Rotten as the State administration was, sullied with bribery as the Turkish generals had become, the pure simplicity and honesty of the people remained unimpaired even to our days.

What were the elements, and what the characteristic aspects of the culture of the Ottomans? Coming from Central Asia toward the West, they picked up elements of culture from the peoples with whom they came in contact. Islam in its Persianized form and even Shî'ite propensities, and Sufism already organized in fraternities, attracted the imagination of the Turks. Asia Minor had for centuries been the meeting place of various cultural influences; pagan remnants of ancient times, Byzantine, Greek, Seljuk-Persian, amalgamated into something new, in which we can analyze the component parts; but the whole is different and more than the mere agglomeration of elements. Asia Minor became Turkicized during the rule of the Seljuks; and the Kay-Khanli newcomers, whose number hardly exceeded 2,000 horsemen, could rely on an adequately large number of Turks to be used as a national reservoir for military expeditions and for colonizing the newly conquered territories. Polygamy did very good service to the Turkish people, as the immense sacrifices of constant warfare could be repaired by a speedy increase. And still the Turkish people had never been able to fill those territories with its own kin and to absorb their native populations into one national unit.

The structure of the Turkish State has from the beginning maintained a splendid isolation of the ruling class from the people. Nationalism in our modern sense has not entered into the mind of the people, and while Arabic Islam has, by propagating the faith, Arabicized foreign races, the Turks did not Turkicize the Balkans, where they were only settlers and did not build up a uniform *nation* even in Anatolia. A strange duality characterizes the Turkish State structure, which cuts across the ties of blood and seems to observe the bonds of the Islamic religion only in the service of the Sultân. The service of the Sultâns admitted under the formality of conversion to Islam any foreign element to the government. This was an inducement to amalgamation and in the history of the Ottomans voluntary acceptance of the faith has largely contributed to the ranks of the ruling class. The heavier burdens imposed on Christians might have moved the agricultural tenants also to enter the fold of Islam. So in Central Anatolia the Karamans, the Western Anatolians, are not Turkish in blood but have become Turkish by religion and then by language also. The Turks, when they set up their empire, conformed to their eclectic activity in administration, which was carried on almost wholly by converted Muslims. An artificial ruling class came into existence which, irrespective of blood, was Islamized in the service of the Sultân. As time and conquest went on this class became more numerous and further removed from the people. It is a strange paradox that the Turkish people, which had excelled from time immemorial in conquest and administration, created a conquering army and an administrative body out of non-Turks who considered themselves alien and superior to the Turkish people themselves. They called themselves Osmanli, a characteristic appellation which meant the adherents of the dynasty of Osman, and despised the common people, whom they called *Turk.* At the head of this official classes of the *Osmanlis* stood the Sultân, the ruler and the unconditional owner of the lives and wealth of the people. The idea of this autocracy was the embodiment of fatherly care and absolute power of disposition over the forces of the people for the common benefit. It reflects the idea of an army where the commander provides the necessaries for the forces and disposes of them according to his insight. The people were his slaves. In the beginning leaders like Osmân, Orkhân, and Murâd bore the old Turkish title: *Bey;* it was Yildirim [Bâyezîd I] who took the titles of *Sultân* and *Khan.* The fatherly tendency of the Turkish rule is shown by the simple habits which the first Sultâns observed. They followed in their habits the old customs of the people. It was with aggrandizement in territory and the increase of palace officials that pomp and luxury and the separation of the Sultân from his advisers set in. Until Muhammad II the Sultân sat among his Vezîrs in council. Once a peasant entered the hall with some complaint "Which of you is the Sultân?" he exclaimed. From that time on the Sultân sat behind the window and listened to the discussion of his advisers. From the time of Süleymân onward the Chief Vezîr reported the decisions of the council to the Sultân, who did not condescend to attend it any more. His will was the last decision and it is strange to notice that with the decline of the empire, as province after province was severed, the haughtiness and seclusion of the Sultâns increased, and at the same time the mischievous influence of a rotten and demoralized palace gained mastery over their will. The first warlike Sultâns transmitted their spirit and their inheritance to their sons; from Ahmed I the law of inheritance was altered and the succession to the throne was continued in the eldest member of the family.

The imperial council, which was the advising body to the Sultân, consisted of the Grand Vezîr (Sadr A'zam), the two Qâzi-askers, the Qâdi of Constantinople, the commander of the Janissaries, the Nishânjî (keeper of the Seal), the treasurer, and the commander of the regiments. The council met every day in the morning and began with proposals and reading of documents by the Reis ül-küttâb. The decisions were protocoled by the Hojegyân and forwarded to the respective officers. The council was the final forum for important law cases also. After the meeting, the Sultân received his Grand Vezîr separately and the other Vezîrs in a body, and listened to their proposals. Appointments and investitures with the robe of office also took place on this occasion. This procedure fell into decay in the seventeenth century, and the meeting took place only occasionally, in the palace of the Grand Vezir or of the Sheykh ül-Islâm. When Mahmûd II tried to restore order in the administration by appointing Ministers, they had to meet twice a week under the presidency of the Grand Vezîr. The Vezîrs received, as a sign of their dignity, three horsetails; the Grand Vezîr was honored by four; before the tent of the Sultân seven standards of horsetails were set up. The retinue of a Vezîr consisted sometimes of several thousands.

As to the technicalities of the Ottoman administration the civil, military, and judicial branches were pretty well mixed; but still there was some attempt at classification. The empire was divided into *vilâyets, sanjaks,* and *kazas.* The heads of the *vilâyets* and *sanjaks* were at the same time military officers, surrounded by a military retinue, and in case of war led the regiments supplied by the feudal chiefs. The head of a *sanjak* was authorized to employ the emblem of one horsetail, the head of a *vilâyet* two. Above the *beys* of Anatolia (Asiatic Turkey) and Rumelia (European Turkey) there were two *beylerbeys* respectively, who at the same time acted as commanders of the army corps. If the command of the two flanks was not entrusted to the royal princes these two beylerbeys led them on the battle-field. These important administrative posts were filled by the system called *devshirme,* which meant the carrying off of Christian children from the Balkans and elsewhere, and educating them in Islam and for their special duties. They were closely attached to the person of the Sultân.

As to the other important posts we may mention the office of the Diwan, which registered the decision of the councils and forwarded it to the respective offices; the land registry (*defter-i haqani*), and the treasury. The head of the Diwan was the Reis ül-küttâb or chief scribe who executed the correspondence with the legations and took part in international negotiations.

One of the most important offices was that of the Nishanji or registrar who issued assignments of land, sealed imperial decrees, and registered newly conquered territories. The Defterdar corresponded to a finance minister. First there was only one; later the European and Asiatic provinces each received one defterdar. They controlled taxation and expenditure.

The class which in Islamic countries played the greatest role, that of the learned (*'ulema*) was instituted by Muhammad II. At the beginning their duties were restricted to the army, as army judges (*kazi-asker*) and up to the end of the fifteenth century there was no independent post for a chief mufti. It was customary to transfer this duty to the kadi either of Brûsa or Constantinople, or to any other learned man who was subservient to the will of the Padishah. By this system of appointment of an official mufti the independence of this important factor of legislation greatly suffered and, while some steadfast Sheikh ül-Islams were capable of checking the extravagance of the Sultâns by their word of veto, the majority were feeble tools in their hands and used to give fatwas which were not in accordance with the spirit of the Sheri'at.

The class of "The Learned" constituted the purely Islamic element in the Turkish ruling society. Their members were not recruited from Christian children kidnapped in the occupied lands, but were descended from Turks and Arabs, and later formed a kind of opposition to the officials of foreign blood. The fear of interference in their authority on the part of the Sultân or the army led to the custom of preserving the profession in the family; and so children were already called *'ulema* in their cradle (*beshik 'ulemalighi*). This abuse, which originated in self defense against encroachments of officialdom, greatly deteriorated the learning and honor of the 'ulema.

By the nature of the Ottoman State the most important class and the mainstay of its power was the army. The Ottoman State, when it was still a village community in Bithynia, relied on its military organization in the feudal system which, similarly to that of the West, enjoined military duties on the holders of fiefs. Very early in the fourteenth century Orkhân and Murâd I, in order to free themselves from the caprices of their feudatories, and in order to control any insubordination, resorted to a plan which immediately elevated the Ottomans to the rank of the first fighting power of the world. A new army, *yeni cheri,* was instituted. A popular legend brings the establishment of this standing army into connection with the antinomian dervish fraternity of the Bektashis; but recent research has proved that the Bektashis slunk into the barracks of the Janissaries in the sixteenth century only, when they tried to free themselves from suspicion of heresy.

The Janissary force was a physically and morally indomitable, absolutely reliable army of unfortunate men who, kidnapped as children, had been brought up in austere surroundings, where they did not know the love of parents or the longing for a fatherland. The only morale they were taught was obedience to their master, the only ambition they fostered was that of promotion and riches. Such a reckless band of men was well fitted to conduct the conquest of empires. The new army could roughly be divided into seven classes, all of which were slaves of the palace (*qapu qulu*), who were stationed in barracks and received a fixed salary and daily allowances from the imperial treasury. The bulk of this regular army was formed of infantry. It consisted of 196 battalions; the strength of a battalion varied from 60 to 2,000 men in different times. The war footing of the Janissary was in the time of Muhammad II some 12,000, in the time of Muhammad III 40,000; and it reached its greatest strength during the rule of Selîm III, when it comprised 110,000 men. Their dress varied in color according to the regiment and the service, and their regiments chose signs such as keys, a fish, or ship's anchors, which were painted on their flags and often tattooed on their arms and calves. Regimental musicians accompanied them and the military ceremonies, traditional to Janissaries, were performed. The daily wage of a Janissary was one *aqche,* a coin containing one-third of a dirhem of silver, at the time of Orkhân, which rose in the course of time to five or six aqche, while some who distinguished themselves received even up to eight aqche. Later, when, through the maladministration of finances, the silver coins were adulterated and lost part of their value, the daily wage was raised accordingly to twenty aqche. Besides these wages each battalion received its regular supply of bread, fat, millet, candles, and uniforms. Their rations were paid every three months. The payment of rations was effected on a Tuesday, before the great hall of the council chamber. The battalions strode up in military order, saluted the Grand Vezîr and his retinue and then at a sign given by the hem of their commander's robe, sat down to eat the food (soup, rice, and meat) prepared for them in the kitchen of the palace, the acceptance of the food signifying their obedience to their master. After taking their meal they again gathered before the hall, whereupon their captains shouted out the *gülbank* (war cry), crossing their arms on their breasts:

> Allah, Allah, no God besides him! With bare head and pure breast take blood, my sword! Many heads are rolled off here and nobody asks why. By God, our force and our sword bring loss to the enemy; our servitude belongs to the Sultân. Threes, sevens, forties, the Mohammedan war cry, the light of the Prophet, the generosity of 'Alî, to our *pir* and master Hâji Bektashi Veli we shout "Hûa!"

After this, at a given sign, the soldiers all rushed to assigned spots where they seized leather bags full of coins which they took to their barracks and distributed. From this ceremony the 65th battalion was excepted, for this battalion was suspected of having been an accomplice in the murder of Prince Osmân. As the Sultân himself was considered a member of the first battalion of Janissaries, he too betook himself after a few days to the barracks in the dress of the Janissaries, took his salary and accepted a glass of *sherbet,* sitting on horseback at the gate, from the hands of the commander, showing thereby his perfect trust in their fidelity.

This closed body of troops did not admit anybody into its ranks who had not special antecedents. Their *esprit de corps* was unshaken by their homogeneous structure; and only at the end of the sixteenth century could jugglers and clowns be added to their ranks as a reward for their services at imperial entertainments. From this time on all kinds of unreliable external elements slipped into the Janissary barracks, dissolved the old bonds and ruined the morale. The Janissaries began to marry, lodged outside the barracks, and pursued some trade in time of peace. The formerly intrepid and austere troops gradually changed into a turbulent, riotous mob which endangered the tranquillity of the realm, while it became useless on the battlefield; and, after several attempts at reorganization failed, it had to be destroyed in 1826.

Besides the standing army there was an equally strongly organized force in the feudal landlords, the *timar* and *ziamet* and *khas* who, according to the extent of their territory, sent well equipped and trained soldiers, infantry and cavalry, to the camp. At the height of the Ottoman power it could raise without any extra expense a cavalry force of 140,000 sabers. No European power up to the Napoleonic wars could muster a force so terrific. The feudal lords received their fiefs as reward for services to the Sultân; some of them were given for a lifetime, some in perpetuity but transferable at decease. While in Europe feudalism, by its inalienable hereditary rights, soon became a danger to the central government, in Turkey the feudal chiefs were always dependent on their overlords. The strength which the Ottoman Empire derived from its feudal system was weakened by the general decay and laxity of morals. The influence of women in the palace invested many unworthy elements with possessorial rights; many feudal lords spent their time far from their estates. It became the custom to farm out the estates, and this was the ruin of most of them. A reckless exploitation of the soil was soon followed by barrenness and lack of produce, and led to a general impoverishment of the country.

The Janissaries and the *sipahi* feudal cavalry formed the bulk of the army; for reconnoitering and other minor services irregular or temporarily engaged troops were utilized. These were armed with rifles, or laid mines and dug ditches around the camp and in fortresses. Most of them were Christians, as those auxiliaries which had to be supplied by the subdued Balkanic peoples.

Turkey, which commanded the whole Mediterranean in the sixteenth century, produced a galaxy of victorious sea-captains like Khaireddin Barbarossa and his son Hasan, Piale, Torgud, Salih Reis, and Piri Reis. The first *tersana* or ship-yard was established at Gallipoli, which was, under the reign of Süleymân [1520-66], transferred to the Golden Horn. The Kapudan Pasha, the chief commander of the fleet, was next in rank to the Grand Vezîr. All the Turkish sea officers and men were sons of Christian parents. Apart from their daring exploits, which terrified Europe, some of them were very able and scientific writers, like Piri Reis, who compiled a sea atlas (*bahriye*) of the Ægean and Mediterranean, every nook of which he had explored, with an account of the currents, soundings, landing-places, and harbors. Another literary seaman was Sîdî 'Alî who was driven ashore in India and traveled back to Turkey by way of Sind, Baluchistân, Khorasân, and Persia. He wrote an account of his three years' journey, and he was the author of a mathematical work on the use of the astrolabe and a book, *The Ocean* (*Muhît*), on the navigation of the Indian seas.

Perfect organization of the work in the shipyards enabled the Ottomans to turn out a fleet fully manned with specially trained sailors and soldiers, a group of which had to serve on the feudal land-tenure system. Slaves, prisoners, and criminals were attached to the mechanical service of the ship, and were treated as galley slaves.

The whole army, in contradistinction to those of other nations, had its peculiar uniform with gaudy colors; close fighting did not necessitate the dissimulation of khaki. Headgear played the most conspicuous part. Bulging trousers with different colored gaiters covering the calves, and heelless high boots buttoned at the side made long and forced marches easy. While marching, the wings of the overcoat were tucked into the belt to give the legs easier play.

The weapons of the Ottomans were a mixture of Asiatic clubs, maces, axes, swords, with European firearms. The first firearms were guns; then came rifles, their first use of which was probably at the battle of Kossowo (1389). But the Ottomans, who utilized the services of foreigners for the improvement of their army, soon outstripped their enemies in casting heavy guns. Revolving guns and a kind of machine-gun were effectively used against attacks of cavalry.

On the declaration of war the different contingents gathered at appointed places. In campaigns toward the West the line of march was Adrianople, Sofia, Nish, Belgrade; toward Russia, Adrianople, Sofia, Badadagi, Irakchi, and along the Dniester. Certain trunk roads had to be followed in order to secure food supply for the troops, and these fixed lines predetermined the places of combat, which were large plains with surrounding hills which each party tried to occupy. The Turkish armies had to keep to certain lines of alimentation. The army started on a campaign accompanied by an immense retinue of caterers, workmen, singers, and jugglers. The camp of a Turkish army presented the most picturesque sight imaginable. Races and costumes from all parts of the world, the whole bazaar of an Eastern town with its manifold products and entertainments, marched along with the fighters. The East marched up and down to Vienna across the Balkans innumerable times.

The tactics of the Turks were naturally based on their military system and have till modern times borne the imprint of the life on the Central Asiatic steppes. Originally it was the tactical deployment of the ancient Persians, who developed a system of cooperation between cavalry and infantry, which system was followed by the Turanian peoples. The battle array was based on a strong center of infantry protected in front by artillery and on the flank by strong squadrons of cavalry. The attack was begun frontally by daring skirmishes of irregular cavalry (*akinji*) who feigned discomfiture and fled in dismay and dragged the vainglorious pursuers into the semicircle of the artillery, which suddenly opened fire on them as the flying irregulars deployed right and left while the flanking cavalry scattered them by encircling movements and the steadfast Janissary infantry rolled them up. The defeated enemy was hotly pursued, and annihilated. These tactics, successfully carried out, resulted in complete victory and the enemy succumbed entirely. One encounter decided the fate of kingdoms. The Turks are born soldiers and in the nineteenth century, when European civilization created long distance firearms and accordingly the traditional tactics had to be abandoned, the Turks easily adopted the new system, in which too they proved equal, if not superior, to any nation. Islam gained its bravest fighters in the Turks, and they are still productive of military genius.

Finance was the weakest point of the Ottoman Empire. As if soldiers were by nature no economists, they could not balance the income and expenses of the State. There was no regular budget, and the whim of the Sultân could destroy the soundest basis of finance. The income of the State was, according to the Muslim law, a tenth, the salt dues, the capitation tax and the purses given by subdued or auxiliary powers, and one-fifth of the spoils. In the period of ascendency the income far exceeded the expenditure. Then it became the custom to distribute large sums to the Janissaries and the palace expenses rose to an uncontrollable height. No regular bookkeeping was established, the provinces were ransacked and impoverished, and with the advent of the new era the purely agricultural Turkey had to purchase industrial articles from abroad. With Süleymân the Great, Turkey standing at the height of its power, financial difficulties already set in. Feudal tenures were converted into *waqf* and the system of farming revenues was introduced. The first attempt at a budget was made in 1609; another in 1653, and another in 1660. At this time the brilliant administration of the two Köprülüs restored temporary order to finance. The form of budget remained the same till 1862, when Fuad Pasha attached a regular budget to his report on the financial situation. The budgets were never accurate; and debased currency and confiscation of property to which the government resorted destroyed public confidence.

A more reassuring aspect is presented if we turn our attention to learning and art, to the contribution of the Turks to Islamic culture in the purest sense. The Turks were always great admirers of learning and faithful pupils of other nations, even though they lacked originality. Their scholars were erudite in Persian and Arabic culture; and, as learning in the Middle Ages was synonymous with theology, the Islamic theology soon captivated the Muslim Turks. Their first Sultâns erected mosques, and at their sides *madrasahs,* where, in the Arabic style, pupils squatted before the columns and went through the curriculum of learning. Those who needed higher knowledge visited the famous schools of Egypt. The language of instruction being Arabic, as Latin was in Europe, an internationalism within the respective cultures was much more general than today, when national languages seem to erect stiff barriers. After the first learned Turks like Sheikh Edebali, the father-in-law of Sultân Osmân, Dursun Faqih and Chandarali Kara Halil, the school of Iznik gained reputation, and this madrasah was founded by Orkhân. After the conquest of Adrianople and Constantinople, wonderful great mosques and madrasahs were erected by the Sultâns; that of Adrianople built by Selîm, and in Constantinople the great Suleymânîyeh were foremost among the seats of learning. Scholars and students flocked there from abroad. The most famous teachers were Aksarayli Jemâluddîn and Sa'aduddîn Taftazânî, whose commentaries are still in use in Muslim schools. Sheykh Bedruddîn wrote valuable books on Sûfism, and distinguished himself from his contemporaries by his liberal philosophic tendencies. Under the reign of Muhammad the Conqueror Mulla Khûsrev distinguished himself by his juridical works, one of which *Ghurar* served as a text for *fiqh,* the other *Durar* as a commentary on it.

During the reign of Selîm I, Zembilli 'Alî Jemâli and Kemâl Pashazâdeh, the great *mufti,* attracted many learned men to their seats, while the reign of Süleymân can boast of Abû Su'ud Efendi and Ibn Kemâl. The latter excelled in commentaries and scholasticism, and also wrote history and poetry. His was a universal talent and he was considered the greatest scholar of his age. Abu Su'ud distinguished himself by his knowledge of the *Sheri'at* of which he was the greatest representative in his age. No Turk could write Arabic as he could. These two great scholars were unsurpassed in later times. With the downward trend of Ottoman power spiritual capacity too seems to have weakened, and although scholasticism prevailed in the Turkish madrasahs up to our days, no new thought, no new departure in philosophy can be noticed. Theological and philosophic learning came to a standstill.

Science in Turkey was first represented by medicine. The lexicon of learned men reveals the names of hundreds of physicians who were of Turkish nationality. The first stone-built hospital was erected by Bâyezîd I (1401) at Brûsa, to which a training college was attached. In the madrasah of the Suleymânîyeh and in the Fâtih mosque the Yunânî medicine was industriously studied. It is noteworthy that, while the medium of theological and philosophical learning was Arabic, books of medicine were written in Turkish. The Turks contributed to the advancement of the medical knowledge of brain diseases and studied the laws of inherited diseases. Among their famous physicians in the time of Bâyezîd were a certain Ishâq and Haji Pasha who wrote learned treatises; in the reign of the Conqueror flourished Altinjizâdeh, Kahwejizâdeh Ahmed, 'Alî Ahmed Chelebi, Vesim 'Abbâs, and others. Their fame and skill in operations, especially as opthalmologists, reached Central Europe. Besides theology and medicine, historiography was a remarkable achievement in Turkish culture. Although as a rule the prose literature cannot compare favorably with the poetical productions of the Turks, the best, and from a scientific point of view the most valuable, of their productions, is their *tarikh* literature. In the beginning it was an imitation of Persian models; later it never quite could get rid of a floridity of style which obscured the meaning. The Sultâns encouraged historiography, for it immortalized their glorious deeds, and though most histories were composed with the one-sided view, with the help of textual criticism the tarikhs still yield valuable information.

The first Turkish historian was 'Ashiq Pashazâdeh who flourished during the reign of Bâyezîd II, and like his contemporary Neshri in his *Jihan-numa* used a fluent and matter-of-fact style in describing the battles of the Ottomans. Idrîs Bitlisî compiled in Persian under the title *Hesht Bihisht,* a historical work in a literary style. The Turkish historians of the fifteenth and sixteenth centuries depict the events before the conquest of Constantinople from the point of view of Ottoman imperialism, and are prone to forget that the Turks issued from a village community and could turn their arms against their rivals in Anatolia only after they had attained to world power by the conquest of Constantinople. From the reign of Süleymân onward the tarikhs become rhymed in form and obscure in meaning. Many of them are panegyrics. The series of official chroniclers (Waqa'navîs), begins with Hoja Sa'deddîn (*Taj ut-tawarikh*) who records the events till the time of Selîm II in a turgid and coarse style. Na'ima is the most reliable source of Turkish history, though his style is also far from impeccable. Rashîd Muhammad, Ismaîl 'Asim, 'Izzi Suleymân, Wâsif Ahmed, Muhammad Subhî, Pechewi, Selanikli Mustafa, 'Alî Efendi, Kâtib Chelebi, and Munajjim Bashi all wrote of the changing events of Turkish history. Besides their comprehensive histories, there are a number of valuable monographs on biography, literature and palace-life, like Mustafa Pasha's *Neta'iju'l-wuqu'at,* Ata Bey's *Anderun Tarikhi,* 'Ali Efendi's *Menaqib-i Hunerweran.* The *Nata'iju'l-wuqu'at* does not restrict itself to the narrating of events, but depicts the administration and organization of the Empire. The *Anderun Tarikhi* is a true picture of palace life written in a surfeited, elaborate style which sometimes sinks from literature to a mere jingle of words. The historicocritical work of Kochi Bey gives the most lucid survey of the causes of the decay of the Empire.

From this brief summary I cannot omit the Turkish geographers. The extension of the empire necessitated geographical knowledge and from the sixteenth century onward we find a number of important geographical and nautical works. Besides those mentioned already, there were Sipâhizâdeh Muhammad and Emîr Muhammad ibn Hasan, who wrote the first Turkish description of America at the end of the sixteenth century.

The greatest of Turkish geniuses was undoubtedly Kâtib Chelebi, commonly known as Haji Khalîfah, the author of the encyclopedic work *Kashf uz-Zunun*. He wrote a general geography under the title *Jihan-numa,* and translated from Latin the Atlas Minor, besides compiling books on naval warfare. Râ'if Mahmûd compiled an English geography and atlas during the reign of Selîm III, (1789-1807).

Turkish literature has borne the imprint of the duality of the nation from the beginning. The ruling and educated classes despised the pure and simple language of the people; and gradually an artificial language came into existence, which was surfeited with Persian and Arabic words to such an extent that it became unintelligible to the people. Literature, for the Ottomans, meant only this stilted, artificial style, following Persian models very closely; the inspiration of the people found vent in cradle songs, stories of the *meddah,* and the stage play *Orta Oyunu* which, though influenced by the Byzantine mimes, thoroughly depicted the life and mentality of the common people. The Chinese shadow play, on its long wanderings across Asia, found easy access in its Islamized form to the liking of the people, and on cool evenings, in fragrant gardens, to the accompaniment of the gurgling of the *nargîleh* and the scent of the famous Turkish coffee, the people eagerly listened to, and enjoyed, the dramatic gestures of the *meddah* and his attractive, sometimes ludicrous stories. The harem life produces the rhymed quatrains composed by women (*mani*-verses), and read by them on festive occasions in a joking way. Folk songs in old Turkish meters survived on the lips and in the hearts of the people for centuries, and some fraternities like those of the Yesewis and the Bektashis composed their illuminative songs in Turkish.

But, apart from these scanty remnants, the literature of the learned was foreign in prosody and foreign in sentiments. It slowly accommodated itself to the taste and feelings of the people, as its political importance increased and clamored for recognition. The first and perhaps the greatest literary productions on Turkish soil were the *mesnewis* of Jelâlu'd-dîn Rûmî, composed in Persian. His son, Sultân Veled, wrote in Turkish but used the Persian prosody. When the Ottoman Sultanate established itself, 'Ashiq Pasha wrote his *Gharib-nameh* and Süleymân Chelebi his *Mevludieh* in pure Turkish; but Persian literature soon overwhelmed these vague attempts and at the time of the Conqueror we find already a Persianized Turkish, and the prominence of Persian models. We may broadly say that, whenever a new star arose in Persia, its brilliance was promptly felt in Turkish poetry. The madrasahs with their Arabic teaching also strongly influenced the literary taste of the learned. Turkish literature has become a true depository of ideas from Islamized Iran. A literature of the palace grew up, its themes being Sûfic, its poetical expression that of the moth yearning for the light in which it ultimately burns. The *dîwâns* with their *qasidahs, medhieh, munajat,* and *ghazals* were the fashionable literary forms. In the time of Süleymân the Magnificent this literary school produced its first great representative, Fuzuli of Baghdad, who, in spite of his coarse provincial Turkish, gave evidence of a first-rate poetic talent in his Dîwân and *Leyla ve Mejnun.* He was surpassed, only as far as refinement of language goes, by Bâqî who flourished in the seventeenth century, and who was considered the greatest Turkish lyric poet. In originality Fuzuli was superior. Zâti with his *Shem u Pervane,* Lâmi'i, Rûhî, and Yahya Bey with his *Shah u Geda,* belong to Bâqî's age. Fashion and taste were thorough imitations of Persian models. This imitative and artificial spirit rose to its highest in the seventeenth century. Nefii and his contemporaries saw the greatest beauty of poetry and prose in style as such, and not in the expression of feelings. In this respect Nergisi went so far that his works are more a play on words than poetry.

In the beginning of the eighteenth century it became impossible to read poetry without ample commentaries, so abstruse had its style become. Nedîm, the gayest of lyric poets, writes in a comparatively clear style. Raghib Pasha represents philosophic poetry, Fitnet Hânim the women's sentimentality of that age. The nineteenth century becomes the harbinger of simplicity, and Sheikh Ghâlib (Muhammad Esad)'s *Husn u 'Ishq,* a rhymed story, and his Dîwân are astonishingly free from the turgidity of his predecessors.

The Dîwân literature begins to ebb and Sümbülzadeh Vehbi, Sürûrî, and Izzet Mulla may be regarded as its last representatives. From the time of the great reformer Sultân Mahmûd II, it became generally felt that the mental and physical structure of the Ottoman empire was debilitated. We can notice that the great statesmen of this period, Pertev and Aqif Pashas and later, under 'Abdul Mejîd, Rifa'at and Reshîd Pashas, felt a nausea at the meaningless adorned style of the official documents, and tried to simplify them. The same tendency is noticeable in literature proper. Another great factor which changed the aspect and taste of literature was the influence of Europe, with which Turkey came into more direct touch from the time of Napoleon. A revival of literature followed, which gave great promise.

As said above, the Turks have a rare imitative and adaptive spirit, by which they can easily imbibe the spirit, the productions of other peoples and utilize them for their purposes. Perhaps in architecture the Turks have set up the noblest monuments of this adaptive spirit. Coming through Persia and Syria, the Seljuk Turks carried the Arabo-Persian ideals of art on into Anatolia, where the influence of Byzantium further enriched their materials. The Turkish genius revealed itself not in blindly accumulating these materials and styles, but in the creation from the ingredient materials of a new, typically Turkish, architecture, which unites the beauty and elegance of Arabic, Persian, and Greek art.

The first architectural monuments of Turkey are to be found in Iznik and Brûsa, which for some time was the capital of the nascent State, and these are mainly public buildings in the Seljuk style, mosques, madrasahs, and tombs. The color of the tiles which were used to cover the walls and the cupolas gave them the name of Green Mosques. The Seljuk style elaborated the carving and the ornaments of the doorway. It must be remembered that the colder climate of Asia Minor did not allow open courtyards to be used as praying-places, but the mosque has become a closed-in hall, and doors came into prominence. The Persian fashion of decorating the walls with colored tiles of high perfection was followed in the mosques of Brûsa and Iznik. The size of the buildings was comparatively small and no pillars supported the roof. The Turks could not cover a large space with one cupola so they resorted to multiplication of the cupolas and thereby minimized the space which each of them had to cover. But the cupolas which were all on the same level did not give the impression of height and soon a development set in which elevated the central cupola above the rest.

With the conquest of Constantinople the Byzantine influence which had only indirectly reached the Turks before, makes itself strongly felt. The great empire provided sufficient wealth to erect splendid public buildings, and the rapidly developing social life necessitated other buildings than mosques and tombs, such as public wells, carvanserays, bazaars, and palaces. The Greek church, Aya Sofia, became the model of the Turkish mosque, such as the mosques of Bâyezîd, Shehzâdeh, Süleymâniyeh, Sultân Ahmed, and Yeni Jâmi'. These buildings are characterized by an extremely high central cupola surrounded by a number of small ones supported by mighty round columns. The walls are not so thick and heavy as in the Byzantine buildings. The arches were either round or pointed but always wide, the capitals of columns were worked out into stalactites. The entrance to the mosque was surrounded by a colonnade and behind it the *'imaretkhanah* with its small round cupolas served as rooms for students.

Instead of the golden mosaics and sacred pictures of the Byzantine churches, the inner walls of the mosques were covered with Arabic inscriptions and the lofty names of the four Caliphs. An innovation of the utmost gracefulness was introduced by the Turks, and added new beauty to the Byzantine style: the minaret. The shape of the minaret varies in the Arabic and Persian styles, and the Turks simplified it by creating a smooth, slender, very high tower with a simple roof; only carved balconies like flower wreaths enrich its simplicity.

A palace was built on the site of the Byzantine palace at the point of the protruding peninsula of Stambûl, on the most glorious spot in the world. It has had a long history, for every Sultân added numerous buildings to it. The most remarkable parts are the harem, for its wall tiles and decorations, and the Baghdad-Kyûshk, which was erected by Murâd IV after the recapture of Baghdad. The architects of these buildings were mostly converted Greeks, like the great and most fertile Sînân, who is supposed to have built more than eighty public monuments.

There is one Jâmi' in the Muslim world with six high minarets, that of Sultân Ahmed on the historic square of the Roman hippodrome opposite the obelisk of Theodosius and the relic of the battle of Plataia. Its architect was Muhammad Agha, a pupil of Sînân.

The eighteenth century marks a new period in architecture. At this time public fountains and palaces were built in abundance, but great fires and earthquakes have destroyed a number of them. The graceful fountain of Ahmed III, the fine Nûr-i Osmâni mosque, and the Laleli Jâmi' are glorious monuments. The European rococo style vaguely but unmistakably announces itself on their decorations, and with extreme refinement decadence sets in. The buildings which were erected in the nineteenth century are strongly imitative of European models.

Constantinople, which is situated on the most beautiful spot in the world, soon increased and spread on both banks of the Golden Horn. Houses made of wood with protruding carved balconies looked more like bird cages than human habitations, but added immensely to the romantic and picturesque aspect of the town. The lattice windows which concealed the beauties of the harem gave a mysterious air to the quiet and calm streets. Mighty *konaks* (palaces) of the rich contained carpets and other ornaments of immense value, but even the poorest Turk kept his house clean and richly decorated with rugs.

Family life, as in every Muslim country, was separate as to sexes. The Sultâns, when their power became paramount, did not marry from noble families but selected their wives from those slave girls who bore sons to them. This did not become the custom of the nobles, who strictly adhered to the prescribed ceremonies of marriage, though it was the fashion to keep a large number of slaves.

Social life was separated into two parts. Men amused themselves in coffeehouses, listening to poets or storytellers; women made excursions on Fridays by boat to the beautiful groves of the fresh waters of Constantinople. Recitations and music and the display of gorgeous dresses of silk and furs made such trips a most enjoyable entertainment.

The economic foundation of social life in Turkey was no doubt the land and its products. The fiefs, sublet to the tenants and industriously looked after, secured the food of the people. Besides agriculture, industry, notably those branches of industry which served military purposes and satisfied the wants of oriental life, soon developed, and gave livelihood to the inhabitants of the towns. The artisans were organized in guilds and the different professions derived their origins from certain *pirs*. Evlîa Chelebî, the greatest traveler of the Turks in the seventeenth century, gives a vivid description of a procession of guilds among which many such an occupation figures as would not be permitted today. The bazaars were veritable museums of oriental wares of leather, tin, copper, woven stuff, and silk, produced in Turkey or imported by an extensive system of caravans from every part of the world. Fleets of merchantmen belonging to Genoa and Venice exchanged the goods of Asia and Europe. The Turks did not care much for maritime trade and left it to foreigners or to their Christian subjects.

The Turk was a soldier and administrator, a judge and guardian of law and order. His only riches consisted of real estate or the salary he drew for service. The Christian subjects took to the more profitable pursuits of trade and soon enriched themselves to such an extent as to rouse the jealousy of the Muslims, whose sons bled to death on the battlefield in the defense of the State. The Christians were exempt from military service and the heaviest burden was borne by the Muslim Turks. And these Muslim Turks sustained their burden with a heroism, with a sincere obedience to the word of God worthy of admiration. They were the bravest knights of Islam and perpetuated its culture, its taste in art and literature, and its aspect of life, when no other Muslim race was able to withstand the onslaughts of Europe. They with their achievements have shown an example of endurance and will-power which, if rightly understood and followed on the cultural path, must inspire other Muslim peoples with self-consciousness and self-reliance.

5

THE STATE AND THE INDIVIDUAL IN ISLAMIC LAW

N. J. Coulson

Coupled with the urgent desire for legal reform apparent in many Muslim countries today are cogent reasons for avoiding, wherever possible, any outright break with the traditions of the past or violent reversal of fundamental concepts. With the modern trend towards democratic forms of government, one aspect of western legal systems which is no doubt of particular appeal to many reformers—especially in those Muslim countries whose ultimate constitution is yet to be determined—is the notion of defined liberties of the individual. It might, therefore, be pertinent to make a brief assessment of the relationship between ruler and subject which finds expression in orthodox Islamic legal doctrine.

The basic principle of the limitation of the power of the State by the rule of law finds a full and absolute expression in Islamic constitutional theory. Islam is the direct rule of Allāh. His law, the *Sharī'a,* is the sole criterion of behavior, and the authority of the temporal ruler, whose existence, as the representative of Allāh, is necessary for the general welfare of the community, is derived from and defined by this law. "The law precedes the State, both logically and in terms of time; and the State exists for the sole purpose of maintaining and enforcing the law." [1] In regulating the relationship between ruler and subject within the overall suprem-

Reprinted, with permission, from *The International and Comparative Law Quarterly,* VI, Part 1 (January 1957), 49-60.

[1] H. A. R. Gibb, in *Law in the Middle East,* p. 3.

acy of the law, orthodox or Sunnī doctrine steers a middle course between those of the extremist sects of Islam: between the Shī'a, on the one side, whose infallible Imām, the living repository of the religious law, is an absolute ruler by divine right; and the Kharijīs, on the other side, with their democratic and egalitarian doctrines, whose Imām is simply *primus inter pares,* elected and deposed by the will of the whole community. Sunnī political theory sees the ideal State as a cooperative partnership between governor and governed, both owing a common obedience to the revealed law. And since the duty of the Imām is to govern according to the dictates of the *Sharī'a,* two major qualifications are required of him. In the first place his own behavior must be, outwardly at any rate, in conformity with the law; that is to say, he must possess the quality of *'adāla* or high moral probity. In the second place, he must have a specialist knowledge of the law, the ability to interpret it and apply it; in other words, the quality of *ijtihād*. But in this respect the authority of the ruler is, in principle, no greater than that of any other qualified *mujtahid*.[2] He is in no sense a legal sovereign of the type of the English Parliament, which has the power to make or unmake any law. There can be no legislative power as such in Islam; there can be no change in the existing law, since that law is divinely ordained and valid for all time. If, in most Western systems, politics and society are the architects of the law, in Islam exactly the converse is true. The law is the blueprint to which the structure of society and State must, ideally, conform. As a matter of abstract principle, therefore, Islamic political theory represents an ideal rule of law. From the provisions of the rigid and immutable *Sharī'a* no one—neither the Imām himself, nor any official of State, nor the judiciary—is by privilege exempt.

Yet to represent, in actual fact, a real guarantee of individual liberties, the idea of the rule of law must carry with it certain essential implications. The first of these is, obviously enough, the recognition of certain individual liberties by the law itself. No such recognition is to be found in the *Sharī'a;* and the formulation of a list of specific liberties of the individual as against the State, in the manner, for example, of the American constitution, would in fact

[2] *I.e.,* one who possesses powers of *ijtihād.*

be entirely foreign to its whole spirit. For Islamic religious law sees as its essential function the portrayal of an ideal relationship of man to his Creator: the regulation of all human relationships, those of man with his neighbor or with the State, is subsidiary to, and designed to serve, this one ultimate purpose. A distinction is indeed drawn between the rights of God (*ḥuqūq* Allāh) and the rights of men (*ḥuqūq 'ibād*), but most authorities would regard only property rights as belonging essentially to the latter class; and in any case, on the higher plane, the whole of the *Sharī'a* is *ḥaqq* Allāh, for all rights and obligations are derived from His command. The stress, therefore, throughout the entire *Sharī'a,* lies upon the duty of the individual to act in accordance with the divine injunctions; and since the conscientious application of these divine injunctions is the declared purpose of the political authority, the jurists did not visualize any such conflict between the interests of the ruler and the ruled as would necessitate the existence of defined liberties of the subject. Early doctrine simply stated, as a pious ideal, that the Imām who ordered something contrary to the *Sharī'a* thereby forfeited his right to the obedience of his subjects and could be deposed. When the texts do assert the principles of "original freedom" and the inviolability of property, life and honor they treat them as principles which secure the general order and well-being of the whole community—the purpose and the right of Allāh—and not as fundamental liberties of the individual.

Because a properly constituted political authority, representing the rule of divine wisdom, guarantees the welfare of the subject in this world and in the world to come, it follows that the interests of the State and not those of the individual will constitute the supreme criterion of the law. This is particularly endorsed by the Mālikī school which formally stresses the principle of *istislāḥ,* or the public welfare, as one of the sources of law. Arguing that each and every disposition of the Lawgiver was designed to secure the welfare of the majority, the Mālikīs claim that cases not specifically regulated by the Lawgiver Himself must be determined by reference to the public interest. From this point of view, then, Islamic legal theory appears much closer akin to the principles upon which Plato's Republic was founded than to the modern

Western ideal which considers "the evolution of the individual as the ultimate measure of things." [3]

Based upon this assumption of the identification of the purposes of God and the ruler is the *Sharī'a* doctrine of *siyāsa,* which allows to the ruler wide discretionary powers to safeguard the interests of the State. *Siyāsa* (government, administration) in its widest sense has, according to Ibn Farḥūn,[4] six purposes: the protection of life, lineage, mind, character, and property, and the elimination of any "corruption." These purposes are achieved by putting into effect the relevant dispositions of the Lawgiver and, where no specific ruling exists, by the exercise of discretion on the basis of the general principles of the law. Theoretically, then, the ruler is not an entirely free agent in this respect, for the only legitimate *siyāsa* is *siyāsa Sharī'a, i.e.,* such discretionary action as secures the public interest and follows the general nature of precedents established by the Prophet himself and the rulers of early Islam. Nevertheless, the doctrine is, in fact, tantamount to a direct negation of what may be regarded as the second essential implication of the idea of the rule of law in secular systems—namely, the principle that the sovereign must not possess any arbitrary power over the subject. And that the doctrine of *siyāsa* and the notion of individual liberty are indeed mutually exclusive will become apparent from a brief analysis of the scope and nature of the discretionary powers which the ruler is held to enjoy in regard to the administration of justice.

To deal first with matters of procedure, the strict *Sharī'a* rules of evidence, which in general terms limit legal proof to the oral testimony of two witnesses possessing the quality of *'adāla* (probity) and, failing such proof, give effect to the defendant's oath of denial, are scarcely suited to the effective maintenance of law and order. Recognizing the need for these rules to be supplemented, particularly in criminal matters, by other "extra-*Sharī'a*" methods of procedure, the jurists admit the power of the ruler to employ such methods as the use of threats or the extortion of confessions by corporal punishment and imprisonment, finding the necessary

[3] Wolfgang Gaston Friedmann, *Legal Theory,* London, 1953, p. 478.
[4] Ibn Farḥūn, *Tabṣirat al-ḥukkām* (Cairo, 1937), II, 133f.

authority in the practice of the early Islamic rulers. The Caliph 'Alī, it is alleged, in order to discover the truth of the plaintiff's claim that he had been rendered dumb as the result of an assault, ordered that his tongue should be pierced with a needle: if red blood appeared the plaintiff was lying, but if the blood was black he was indeed dumb. All such stratagems are, according to Ibn Farḥūn, "good *siyāsa*." [5]

In sum it appears that where the normal rules of procedure are ineffective the ruler is allowed to adopt, within reason,[6] any method he sees fit to discover the facts of the case. Particularly harsh treatment is recommended for the individual of reputedly bad character whose guilt is suspected but cannot be proved in the orthodox fashion. He should be subjected to rigorous examination, with beating and imprisonment if necessary, for "were we simply to subject each suspect to the oath and then free him, in spite of our knowledge of his notoriety in crime, saying: 'We cannot convict him without two '*adl* witnesses,' that would be contrary to *siyāsa Sharī'a*." [7] Nor, in the event of the subsequent release of the suspect, is there any question of a remedy for malicious prosecution or false imprisonment. It is only where no proof is forthcoming and the person charged is of such high repute that none would normally suspect him of the alleged offense that the accuser will be punished.

Equally extensive is the scope allowed to the discretion of the ruler in the determination of offense and sanction. Apart from homicide the *Sharī'a* specifies only six[8] offenses to which are attached defined penalties (*ḥadd,* pl. *ḥudūd*). Other offenses may be either of the same essential nature as the *ḥadd* offenses but of a less serious degree or may qualify simply as "corruption"; in the latter case the determination of the offense itself and in both cases the determination of the punishment are matters for the discretion of the Imām. Some evidence is afforded by the texts of a desire on the part of the jurists to make other offenses and their sanctions more specific. Thus,

[5] *Tabṣirat,* II, 138-141.

[6] The use of methods expressly prohibited by the *Sharī'a,* such as mutilation by torture, would, of course, be wholly illegitimate.

[7] *Tabṣirat,* II, 154f.

[8] Illicit sex relations, slander, theft, wine drinking, armed robbery, and apostasy.

for example, in dealing with defamatory statements other than the false accusations of unchastity or illegitimacy which entail a *ḥadd* penalty, certain jurists would prescribe twenty-five lashes for calling a person "a criminal" or "a wrongdoer," ten lashes for calling a Muslim "a Jew," and ten, fifteen, or twenty-five lashes for a false imputation of theft.[9] But these attempts to systematize are spasmodic, and the suggested penalties, though some of them appear to have won fairly wide acceptance, are in the main quoted as simple illustrations and guides. They are not authoritative in the sense that they qualify the general principle that, outside the *ḥadd* offenses, "punishment depends entirely on the personal opinion of the Imām." [10]

The Imām, however, "must not pronounce penalties at his mere whim or pleasure or turn from one to the other in an arbitrary fashion: for this would be injustice and contrary to *ijmā'*." [11] His decision must be the result of conscientious reasoning (*ijtihād*) on the basis of the general principles of the law as enunciated in the authoritative texts.

Penalties imposed at the discretion of the ruler (or the judge) are known as *ta'zīrāt*. The term *ta'zīr* has the root meaning "to prevent," and the jurists repeatedly stress the fact that the primary purpose of the *ta'zīrāt* is to serve as a correction for the offender himself and a deterrent for others. In contrast, therefore, with the *ḥadd* offenses or the offense of homicide, the sanctions of which are of an essentially retributive nature, the extent of the *ta'zīrāt* must differ according to the nature of the offense, the character of the offender and, where applicable, the character of the victim.

Most jurists, however, accept the principle that *ta'zīr* punishments should be less than those prescribed for the *ḥadd* offenses. Thus, in the Hanafī view, the maximum number of lashes permissible, where beating is administered as a *ta'zīr* punishment, is thirty-nine, since forty lashes is the *ḥadd* penalty imposed upon the slave for the offense of *qadhf*.[12] Imprisonment, according to

[9] *Ibid.*, II, 308.
[10] *Ibid.*, II, 301.
[11] Qarāfī, *al-Furūq* (Cairo, 1925), IV, 182.
[12] *Qadhf* is the false imputation of unchastity or illegitimacy.

the Shāfi'ī school, should normally be of six months' duration, and even when applied as a preventive measure (where the criminal's behavior is such as to encourage others to do the same) must be for less than one year—for imprisonment is a punishment of the same nature as banishment or exile, and the period of banishment prescribed for the *ḥadd* offense of fornication is one year. For the Mālikīs, on the other hand, the *ta'zīr* punishments are not, of necessity, limited in this way, and the principle that the punishment should fit the crime, the criminal and the victim is of absolute application. Thus the death penalty is permissible in certain cases, where either the offense itself is of a very serious nature, such as spying for the enemy or propagating heretical doctrines or practices which split the community, or the criminal is an habitual offender whose wickedness can only so be stopped, one example given being that of the confirmed homosexual. Although, in regard to beating, individual Mālikī jurists allow maximum figures ranging between seventy and 400 lashes, the dominant doctrine is that the number of lashes will depend entirely upon the discretion of the Imām. In the same way imprisonment may be for a day or for life.

All schools agree that there is no fixed minimum of *ta'zīr* punishment. *Ḥadd* penalties are essentially *ḥuqūq* Allāh and, where the offense is established, must be applied as prescribed. But for other offenses it is not obligatory upon the Imām to impose actual punishment. A simple reprimand or moral exhortation is possible in suitable circumstances—where, for example, the offense is committed in the heat of the moment and is completely unrelated to the general character and behavior of the culprit, or where the offender is unaware of the fact that his behavior is an offense. In principle some punishment ought to be applied if the offense concerns a right of Allāh and a simple reprimand is only permissible in such cases if the Imām is convinced that this will better serve the public interest. Should the offense be considered purely, or at least essentially, as a tort, the injured party may pardon or intercede for the offender, but the Imām is not obliged to accept his plea and may still award some punishment as a matter of public policy. The general tendency, however, is to advocate leniency in deserving cases, and to insist that no more punishment should be applied than is necessary to achieve the objective of correcting the offender. It follows naturally from this fundamental principle that *ta'zīr* punishment is not permissible if the offender shows a true and sincere repentance. "It is better that the Imām should err in pardoning than in inflicting punishment." [13]

Such are the broad limits set by legal doctrine to the discretionary powers of the sovereign. The texts would also restrict the ruler's freedom of choice on many points of detail by formulating, for example, the conditions which determine the applicability of one or other of the alternative penalties prescribed for the *ḥadd* offense of *ḥirāba* (armed robbery), or by specifying the circumstances under which the ruler may give effect to a pardon granted by the victim to one guilty of the offense of *qadhf*. Nevertheless, the whole spirit of the texts is advisory, and such provisions as they contain are offered by way of guidance rather than invested with any compelling authority. Nor must it be forgotten, in this respect, that the *Sharī'a* embodies a wealth of diversity of opinion, and that it is the acknowledged right of the ruler to impose that one opinion among conflicting authorities which he considers best suited to the case in point. Normally, too, the jurists confine themselves to generalizations; here the punishment should be "light" or "moderate"; here it should be "severe" or "painful." The details are almost always left to the ruler's discretion, as also, often, is the form that the punishment should assume. For while imprisonment or beating may be recommended as most fitting in certain cases, it is implied that any reasonable method of punishment which the ruler deems sufficient to secure the intended result will be permissible. Finally, the doctrine of necessity further broadens the scope of the ruler's discretionary powers. "The extent of *siyāsa* regulations must differ as times and circumstances differ. . . . If it is permissible to accept those of immoral character as witnesses owing to the prevailing low standards, it is equally permissible that there should be greater latitude for *siyāsa* rulings on account of the widespread corruption of the times." [14]

In such circumstances the only real and effective liberties which will result from the principles that the subject may do and say

[13] *Tabṣirat,* II, 301.
[14] *Tabṣirat,* II, 151.

what he pleases so long as he does not break the law and that the political authority may do only what is permitted by the law will be those which the political authority itself is prepared to guarantee. Islamic legal doctrine, as has been noted, does not proceed on the basis of a purpose to protect the individual against the State. Concentrating upon the ideal of a government wholly in accordance with the letter and the spirit of the divine law, the jurists completely subordinate the principle of the individual liberty to that of the public interest and welfare. For under this ideal form of government, they argue, all men will naturally receive their due rights. The supreme paradox, which leads to an outright nullification of this pious ideal, lies in the fact that the *Sharī'a* fails to provide any guarantee that government will, in practice, assume this ideal form, and that, far from ensuring the existence of practical remedies against the ruler's abuse of his recognized powers, it simply counsels acceptance of such abuse.

The first centuries of Muslim history had adequately demonstrated the evils of civil discord and strife (*fitna*), and it was the fear and abhorrence of *fitna* which dominated legal thought: "Sixty years of tyranny," runs a tradition, "are better than one hour of civil strife." [15] Conscious of the lack of any effective constitutional procedure for implementing the pious ideal that the ruler who contravenes the dictates of the divine law ought to be deposed, later jurists advocated that, in the interests of the community as a whole, allegiance should be given to the existing authority, of whatever nature it might be. "An evil-doing and barbarous Sulṭān," stated the theologian Ghazzāli, "must be obeyed." Though the unjust ruler would be punished in the world to come, the subject had no present remedy against the abuse of autocratic power, for his obligation to obey the established authority rested upon the text of the Qur'ān itself: "Obey Allāh, his apostle and those at the head of affairs." [16]

Obedience is not required from the subject if this would constitute a *ma'sīya,* that is to say, if the ruler should command that which is expressly prohibited by the law or prohibit that which is obligatory. But, this apart, no form of opposition, from criti-

[15] See Gibb in *Law in the Middle East,* 15-18.
[16] Qur'ān, IV, 61, 62.

cism or abuse of the leaders to open and armed revolt, is to be tolerated. Insisting that the primary consideration must be the internal peace and order of the community, the jurists take a most serious view of all activities which might hamper or obstruct the ruler in the realization of his paramount duty, and, in brief, allow him a practically absolute discretion in dealing with elements of opposition. Such powers, originally afforded to the ruler by virtue only of his being ideally qualified to rule according to the dictates of the law itself, are, by reason of political necessity and expediency, admitted as belonging to the ruler who is by no means so qualified; and thus the religious law, its whole moral basis destroyed, comes to admit and tolerate secular absolutism.

This failure to translate into actuality the ideal of the rule of law results from the absence, in Islamic legal theory and practice, of what must be, ultimately, the only real guarantee of individual liberty in any system, namely a powerful and independent judiciary. And this situation, in turn, is the natural result of the fundamental nature and the historical development of Muhammadan religious law.

The elaboration of *Sharī'a* doctrine was the result of a speculative attempt by pious scholars, working during the first three centuries of Islam, to define the will of Allāh. In self-imposed isolation from practical needs and circumstances they produced a comprehensive system of rules, largely in opposition to existing legal practice, which expressed the religious ideal. But they neglected to ensure that the independence which they enjoyed in their deliberations would also be enjoyed by those charged with the task of applying this law in practice. Instead they accepted the existing system of the administration of justice, under which the judge, or *qādī,* was merely the legal secretary of the political authority.

Islamic political theory is not based upon the principle of the separation of powers. Supreme executive and judicial power is vested in the sovereign, and by the process of delegation each and every official of State becomes his representative. Judicial competence results only from appointment by the ruler. The *qādī,* therefore, is subordinate to and subject to dismissal by the established political authority; in relation to that authority he is "as the part is to the whole." At the same time the *qādī* is the only fully qualified representative of the *Sharī'a,* and, as such, is not, theoretically, subject to any interference or influence of the political authority in deciding the cases that come before him. But the jurists admit the right of the ruler to restrict the competence of his *qādī* by forbidding him to hear certain classes or types of cases; and further they recognize the fact that in the majority of instances the *qādī* is entirely dependent upon the political authority for the execution of his judgments. For the *qādī's* responsibility ends with the pronouncement of the judgment and he has not, in theory, the power to execute his judgments unless this is expressly included in the terms of his appointment or permission to such effect is granted by the ruler in the individual case.

Since, moreover, it was perfectly legitimate for the ruler to delegate full or limited judicial competence to officials of State other than the *qādī,* the jurists were forced to recognize the so-called extra-*Sharī'a* tribunals. Summary jurisdiction, for example, normally belongs to the police in criminal cases, and the various departments of governmental administration enjoy judicial competence in cases which concern their particular sphere of activity. These and other courts are not bound by the strict *Sharī'a* rules of procedure and their decisions are admitted to be valid provided they do not flagrantly contradict the general principles of the religious law. The texts as a rule deal only with the broad principles of administrative law, and where in fact they go beyond this must be considered illustrative rather than fully or universally authoritative. For in the event the powers and functions of the executive authorities will depend upon the discretion of the ruler. "Appointments differ on the basis of local custom and the terms of the individual appointment. . . . Neither for general nor for particular appointments does the *Sharī'a* define the terms."[17]

It is scarcely surprising, in the circumstances, that the *Sharī'a* does not provide any real system of organized appeal; and in fact in no case does the right of appeal exist as such. Apart from the possibility of a judge revising a decision of his own or reversing the decisions of his predecessor in office, the jurists are concerned

[17] *Tabṣirat,* II, 141, 158.

only with the case of a complaint to the ruler which results in the punishment or deposition of the judge concerned and the amendment or annulment of his judgment. Here, as throughout the whole system of the administration of justice, the doctrine is based upon the assumption of the ideally qualified ruler. Pious declarations may be found to the effect that the ruler must depose those officials who are suspected of injustice and severely punish the judge who has abused his judicial power, but once the moral basis of the structure collapses no sure and effective remedy for injustice exists. Nor is there any such system as "droit administratif" to provide a real remedy against the abuse of individual rights by governmental administrative bodies. Islamic jurisprudence ideally rejects the possibility of any conflict between the interests of the executive and those of the law, and, should this occur, sees as the only remedy the application of the religious law by the ordinary courts. But it is clear that political interests and power may well render ineffective any remedy for the injustice of officials emanating from courts which are dependent upon the political authority for the execution of their judgments. Furthermore, as has already been shown, the doctrine itself abandons its moral and religious foundations in the face of political necessity. "If the Imām orders a wrong[18] and to disobey the order would foment a split in the community, then the order must be obeyed, . . . for the *Sharī'a* prohibits the toleration of civil strife."

No adequate machinery, therefore, is provided by the legal theory to protect the individual against the State. Indeed the whole spirit of the religious law is fundamentally opposed to the notion of an independent judiciary fearlessly defining the limits of the power of the State over the individual and powerful enough to give effect to its decisions. The theory proceeds on the assumption that the *qādī* will perform his office in ideal circumstances, supported, that is, by the religious morality of the ruler and the great mass of the subjects. As the subordinate of the ruler the *qādī* should attempt in all humility to apply the *Sharī'a,* assuming the role of arbiter rather than judge. His duty is to settle disputes by reconciliation of the parties if possible, rather than by asserting where the right lies;

[18] Provided, that is, that it does not amount to a *ma'siya*. See above, p. 130.

for, conscious of human fallibility, he should hesitate to define the law of Allāh with certain and definite authority. "The person who knows a judgment to be wrong must not give it effect. . . . The Prophet said: 'I am a man. . . . If I grant to anyone by my judgment a right which is not his, let him not take it.'"[19] It is, in fact, the ruler who must assume the responsibility of executing judgments.

Persisting in this ideal the judiciary found itself powerless to intervene against a ruler who flagrantly violated the principles of the *Sharī'a.* They were forced to the doctrine that to endure such unjust government was to accept the lesser of two evils by avoiding civil strife; for the place and the function which they had assigned to themselves in their scheme of the State afforded them no other alternative.

This is not to deny that there have existed strong and resolute judges who have effected the conscientious application of the divine law in practice. This was the case, for example, in the Ottoman empire, where the *qādī* was the central authority in his area of jurisdiction and the Shaikh al-Islam, at the head of a powerful hierarchy of judicial and theological authorities, had the power to authorize the deposition of the Sulṭān for violation of the sacred law.[20] But such situations are the result of particular circumstances and individual personalities; they cannot serve to effect any change of the basic principles of the doctrine in a system of law which is fixed and unalterable and does not recognize the binding force of judicial precedent. To the power of the ruler who is supported by adequate physical force the *Sharī'a* sets no other limits than those which he finds in his own conscience.

The problem, therefore, which today confronts those Muslim countries whose aim is the establishment of a system of guaranteed individual liberties is no small one. For the possibility of such a system is denied by the fundamental doctrines of the *Sharī'a* itself. Turkey deemed the only practical solution to lie in the abolition of the *Sharī'a* and the secularization of the State. Any Muslim country, however, which might wish to preserve the basic Islamic ideal of

[19] *Tabṣirat,* I, 75.

[20] Bernard Lewis, in *Unity and Variety in Muslim Civilisation,* ed. von Grunebaum (Chicago 1955), 325.

a religious State, wherein all relationships are regulated by the authority of the same religious command, must, perhaps, look to the example set by the new Constitution of Pakistan. Here the doctrines of the medieval texts—hitherto invested with a final and indisputable authority—are abandoned, and a system of fundamental rights is established upon the basis of a new and liberal interpretation of the original sources of Islamic law—the Qur'ān and the traditions of the Prophet. Salutary such a procedure certainly is; legitimate it may be according to the criterions of Muslim legal modernism; but it involves a radical reformulation, to say the least, of traditional Islamic principles.[21]

[21] The method adopted by the constitution makers of Pakistan—namely the reassertion of the right of independent reasoning (*ijtihād*) which has traditionally been inadmissible since the eleventh century A.D.—will, it is hoped, be discussed in detail in a later article.

6

IS THE CALIPH A POPE?

George Stewart

For centuries the Caliphate has been a powerful and mysterious factor in the political and religious life of the Near East. A number of circumstances have conspired to draw attention to this office in recent years.

The Dardanelles disaster, the landing of the Greeks in Smyrna in May of 1919, followed three years later by the Hellenic *débacle* in Anatolia, and the subsequent Turkish victory at Lausanne, the plight of Protestant missions, colleges, and hospitals in Turkey and the menace of the Turkish Nationalist Government to native churches of minority peoples have caused increased consideration of the Caliphate.

Finally the abolition of the Caliphate by Mustafa Kemal Pasha caused queries as to the nature and power of that office which, to the western mind, has symbolized the unity and authority of the Moslem religion.

Mr. Lathrop Stoddard's publications, "The Rising Tide of Color" and "The New World of Islam," vivid, arresting, and valuable as they are, have exaggerated any self-conscious unity of Mohammedanism that may exist, and have created the idea in some quarters that Moslem peoples are held together by an unbreakable spiritual cohesion. Sir Thomas W. Arnold's recent volume,

Reprinted, with permission, from *The Moslem World,* XXI, 2 (April 1931), 185-96.

"The Caliphate," presents a far more adequate treatment, showing clearly that at no time did any Caliph rule over a united Islam.

The Caliphate arose from a series of circumstances vastly different from those which gave rise to the Holy Roman Empire and its institutions. Charlemagne assumed a title held by non-Christian emperors before him, but gave its function a Christian character. In those actions, he was largely influenced by his study of St. Augustine's dream of a Christian commonwealth—*De Civitate Dei.* The office of the Caliphate came into being not from deliberate plan or foresight, but almost from accident. Due to the prostration of the two great rival empires, Persia and Rome, the Arabs—through no spiritual or intellectual renaissance, or military genius—fell heir to vast sections of these former empires, whose military and naval defenses had decayed. Unlike Charlemagne, who copied his Christian Empire from the earlier forms of Roman legal and administrative genius, the Caliphate was moulded by the turbulent accidents of the age that gave it birth.

Later Mohammedan theologians and jurists, *nunc pro tunc,* accredited its rise and power to a theory which had not existed in the beginning, a postulation after the fact.

The theory of the Caliphate was expressed first in the Traditions, which are claimed as the utterances of the Prophet or his immediate associates. These, as is the case of Christian Scriptures, were first oral traditions, and were gradually reduced to writings. The Traditions were rapidly surrounded with a theory of literal infallibility, and are held to be supreme when a question is in dispute concerning the Koran itself.

A second difference exists between the Caliphate and the Holy Roman Empire, in addition to that of origin, and that is in the matter of the spiritual function of the Caliph. Among the Sunni Mohammedans, represented to the western mind principally by Turks and Arabs, divine revelation is held to have ceased with the Koran and the Traditions, the interpretation of which is given to the *'Ulama,* or learned men, and in no respect does interpretation appertain to the Caliph. The Caliph has no spiritual functions and in no sense corresponds to the Pope of the Roman Church, or to the Patriarch, Exarch, or Metropolitan of the Eastern Orthodox Church.

It is true that acting in the capacity of an Imam he may stand before Moslems and lead them in worship, but so may a slave or a camel driver or even the son of a prostitute. No special consecration or ordination is necessary for this office, and Islam has no body of men especially trained and set aside as a priesthood. The authority for interpretation in spiritual matters resides in those laymen who choose to devote themselves to the study of theology, the *'Ulama,* or the learned. This learning, however, does not raise them in rank above the general body of the faithful. But it ought to be stated that among the Eastern Moslems, represented by the Persians, the Imam has great authority as an expounder of sacred writ, this increased prestige of the Imam constituting a radical difference in practice between the Shiahs and the Sunnis.

Islam has no sacraments—no body of specially trained or consecrated men set aside for sacerdotal functions. There is no ecumenical head of Islam, there are no holy orders, no intermediaries. The sole semblance of a priestly group corresponding to clergy that may be found among Moslems is a certain group of small religious fraternities which sprang up six centuries after Mohammed. In these, however, the spiritual bond is between the masters and those who seek their wisdom. Ritual and doctrine are not touched upon, and the fraternities have no formative influence upon theology such as that now exercised by the great writers in the monasteries of the west.

A third distinction exists between the Holy Roman Empire and Islam, and that is, that the former ceased to exist even before Napoleon, in 1806, declared it extinct, while the Caliphate has persisted into post-war times.

Reviewing the history, one pauses to wonder how the Caliphate came into being. Mohammed left no will; he nominated no one to follow in his steps, he delegated no spiritual power, and he did not deliver the keys of the Kingdom of Heaven to an apostle. While he lived, he was the ruler of both a state and a religion, each of which he founded. When he died, his follower succeeded to the worldly power, but not to the spiritual. Islam, placing its faith in Allah and in its sacred writings, has never regarded the Caliph as its spiritual head, but as a symbol of a united worldly Moslem power that has, in fact, never existed. Whatever theory arose regarding the Caliphate was an invention of other minds than that of Mohammed. Upon the Prophet's death, Abu Bakr, Umar, and Abu Ubaydah formulated plans to elect the former as Chief of the Faithful. Word being received by them that the chiefs of the most powerful tribe of Medina, the Banu Khazraj, were about to choose a chief, they hurried to the place of meeting, and succeeded in having their candidate elected by acclamation. The next day, therefore, Abu Bakr took his place on the *mimbar* where Mohammed was accustomed to speak to the people, and upon the call of Umar the people swore allegiance to the new chief.

Abu Bakr held office for two years when, according to tradition, he nominated Umar to follow him, a tribal custom pursued by the desert peoples. With regard to the Caliphate, the theory was clear, that it was this subsequent election by the tribe that constituted the acutal investiture of power.

Tradition holds that Umar, who was stabbed by an assassin ten years later, appointed six electors to choose his successor; but this may be an invention of a later period to explain a procedure arising in other ways. At any rate, a theory of election came into being which has persisted into modern times under the Ottoman Sultanate. The Caliph made his nomination first to a small gathering of powerful men who swore allegiance at that time, and it was this procedure that was followed by public proclamation and the assent of the populace.

The hereditary principle appeared first when Mu'awiyah, the founder of the Umayyad dynasty in 676, four years previous to his death, nominated his son as the future Caliph. This precedent was followed generally in theory during the period of the Abbasid Caliphs. The ablest son was nominated, but, in reality, during the first twenty-four Caliphs holding office from 754 to 974, only six were actually succeeded by a son. The theory of election, however, was not lost during this period.

The equality of all believers was a theory easily maintained while the government remained at Medina, surrounded with associations of the Prophet, but when, in 661, Mu'awiyah removed the seat of government to Damascus, the pride of the Arabs caused them to regard themselves as rulers over subject nations. Little groups of devotees in Mecca and Medina regarded this transformation of the Caliphate, accompanied by a luxurious temporal leadership, with alarm, and protested against it. But before the Umayyad dynasty closed, the Damascus Caliph ruled over an empire that stretched from India and China across Arabia and North Africa, through Spain, and even into modern France. The successors of Mohammed had become powerful secular rulers.

During the Abbasid dynasty, the Caliphs assumed the role of patron of religion in a greater degree than had their less pretentious predecessors, the Umayyads. The latter were easy to approach, and assumed few regal airs; the former surrounded themselves with ceremonious splendor and retained their executioners constantly at hand. Sagacious subjects frequently carried their funeral shrouds with them upon a summons to the palace.

The theory of the Caliphate was elaborated during this period of Arab aggrandizement under the Abbasids, the theorizing process continuing even during the later days of their extreme humiliation. Abu Bakr, successor of Mohammed, took the modest title of Khalifah Rasul Allah—Successor of the Apostle of God. This humble title grew to be a magnificent symbol of power as the result of the overrunning of the broken empires of Persia and Rome by the hungry and vigorous Moslem Arabs.

Umar, in the era of great conquest and expansion, assumed the title of Amir ul-Mu'minin, Commander of the Faithful, and it was by this term—the title Saladin used—that the Caliphs were known to the Christians during the Middle Ages. A third title, Imam, had special reference to the religious functions of leading the faithful in prayer. The earlier Caliphs might be described by either one of the three titles.

In 750 the Abbasids wrested the Caliphate from the Umayyads in the battle of Zab, and for five centuries they held the Caliphate within their immediate family. This family drew the Shiah Mohammedans to their support, pretending a common devotion to the Prophet's family in matters of descent. But the Abbasids claimed allegiance to al-Abbas, the uncle of the Prophet, and not—as the Shiahs held—to the son-in-law of Mohammed. When the Abbasids obtained all they desired from the Shiahs, they deserted them and pursued their own selfish path. The Umayyads preserved the old

Arab culture, tribal customs and loyalties during their reign, but the entrance of the Abbasids marked the shifting of the Arab Kingdom with a Moslem religion to a strict, theocratic Moslem rule.

The highest point of power reached by the Abbasids may be set about the year A.D. 800, the year Charlemagne was crowned in Rome as the first Emperor of the Holy Roman Empire. Dissolution of the Abbasids' power set in quickly, however. An Umayyad prince fled to Spain and declared it a separate kingdom, in 756, while North Africa—for all practicable purposes—became an independent kingdom under the hereditary Aghlabid dynasty from the year 800. Egypt and Syria separated, and Persia came soon to be ruled by a separate dynasty. By the end of the ninth century, Abbasid power had shrunk until its influence was confined almost exclusively to the city of Baghdad. The weakness and licentiousness marking the Caliphate at this time invited aggression, and Caliph Muqtadir (908-32), a drunken and dissolute ruler, first at the mercy of his lawless Turkish mercenaries, after being twice deposed, was slain and his head impaled upon a spear. The Baghdad Caliphate became the victim of one powerful prince after another. At one period there lived three Abbasid princes each of whom in his time had held the office of the Caliphate, and each of whom had been blinded by a powerful ruler and robbed of everything of value. For two centuries, cruel masters, the Buwayhids, were served. These were a Persian dynasty who expanded, and seized Baghdad in 945, under whom the monarch's name was put in the *Khutbah,* or Friday sermon, the symbol of sovereignty, an occurrence which dramatized the lowest depth to which the Caliphate fell under the Abbasids.

It is a fact singularly striking that the greatest treatise on the theory of the Caliphate was written at the time of is utter humiliation, by Mawardi, a jurist who died in 1058 at the age of eighty-six. The jurists have held generally that the following characteristics must be present in order to qualify a candidate for election to the high office of Caliph: he must be a member of the tribe of Quraysh, a male of mature age, of spotless character, without physical or mental infirmity, a man of sound judgment; he must, in addition, possess knowledge sufficient to adjudicate cases at law and must possess courage and energy in the defense of Moslem lands; he must be, at one and the same time, administrator, judge, and general.

With the declination of the power of the Abbasids, the Caliphate became a name only, to which non-Arab rulers gave an indifferent respect for political reasons. Nevertheless, from the founding of the Abbasid dynasty, in the middle of the eighth century, to the death of Musta'sim, the last Abbasid Caliph in 1258, the holder of the office was considered the Commander of the Faithful by all orthodox Sunni Mohammedans. Independent princes, who cared little or nothing for religion, saw to it that the reigning Caliph sent to them a diploma of investiture or a title, in order to satisfy pious Moslems.

The Buwayhid princes, who entered Mesopotamia from Persia and completely dominated the Caliphate from 945 to 1055, gave way to the Seljuk Turks who entered Baghdad in the latter year. These people were a visiting power from Persia who had assumed proportions in Mohammedan history and had built rapidly an immense empire. The Abbasid Caliphate improved under the Seljuks for a time, and, during a period of dynastic warfare among the Turks, a Caliph even ventured to take the field, but was defeated and put to death. The crowning humiliation of the Abbasid dynasty, however, was received when the Mongols, under Hulagu, invaded Baghdad in 1258 and trampled the Caliph to death. Following this for a time the office ceased to exist, to the consternation of the Moslem jurists.

The Abbasids for two centuries during their regime were confronted with rival Caliphates. The Almoravid dynasty, among the Berbers of North Africa, founded a considerable empire, Morocco being the result of their conquests. Finally, in 1086, defeating the Christian armies at the battle of Zallaka, they added the Moslem provinces of Spain to their lands. The Almoravids, however, recognized the Abbasid Caliph and this compensated him somewhat for his feeble position at Baghdad. In 1171, the rival Caliphate of the Fatimids in Egypt came to an end. Saladin, defeating the Franks, displaced the rival Shiah Caliph, who had reigned in Egypt and was a Fatimid, and gave his allegiance to the Abbasid Caliph. Moslem India, represented by the conquest of the Slave kings—so called because they were former Turkish slaves who achieved their office by reason of military prowess—also gave homage to the Abbasid Caliph in Baghdad. These, as other conquerors, found in the diplomas and mantles of the Baghdad Caliph a convenient way to legitimatize their conquests.

The Abbasid Caliphate at Baghdad was now revived in Egypt through the exigencies of the Mamluk rulers who needed sanction for their rule. Consequently, the fourth Mamluk ruler procured an uncle of the last Abbasid Caliph in Baghdad, and set him up in Cairo as Caliph with great pomp and ceremony, although the Caliph remained practically a prisoner in the citadel at Cairo. Thus for two hundred and fifty years, weak and almost helpless Abbasid Caliphs gave a semblance of legitimacy to Mamluk rule in Egypt.

During this period other Moslem princes looked to the almost impotent Caliph for sanction of their rule. The founder of the Muzaffarid dynasty in Persia and the Turkish Sultans of Delhi both found his *imprimatur* a convenient political device. In Transoxiana, Timurlane nominated his grandson to follow him. After the great conqueror's death, the throne was contested, and the grandson advised to apply to the Abbasid Caliph in Cairo for a diploma of investiture, a counsel which he rejected. The Ottoman Sultan, Bayazid I, in 1394, applied to the Caliph for permission to use the title of Sultan. Thus the fiction of a powerful Caliphate was perpetuated through the needs of turbulent princes.

Several Moslem potentates, despising the pretensions of the Abbasids, set themselves up as Caliphs during the period of the Abbasids at Cairo. Abu Abdallah Muhammed (1249-1277) of the Hafsid dynasty in Tunis was one of the first rivals to claim the title. The same occurred in Asia Minor, India, Mesopotamia, and Transoxiana, until the description of Caliph became fairly frequent among Moslem historians. The Mogul emperors of India commonly employed the title for themselves.

Several Ottoman Sultans arrogated the title thus connoting so great an authority. However, the title had been claimed by so many puny rulers that the mighty Ottoman, Sultan Salim, did not employ the term for himself, even after conquering Egypt. A few years before, in 1508, when the Shah of Persia, his rival, had captured

Baghdad from the Turkomans, he appointed a eunuch governor, and dubbed him "Caliph of the Caliphs." Salim achieved his power by his sharp sword, and chose to ascribe it to that instrument rather than to the shadowy authority which the last Abbasid Caliph in Cairo is alleged to have handed on to him when he overran Egypt. Neither did his son, Sulayman, employ the title.[1]

Although the earlier Ottomans took pride in the strength of their arms and used the term Caliph only infrequently for themselves, following 1700, when the powers of western Europe came more and more into contact with the Moslem world, the Turks were astute enough not to overlook the value of such a claim in diplomatic negotiations. Therefore, the false idea arose among Christians that the Caliph was a sort of Pope—a spiritual ruler over a united Islam—an idea that was exploited to the full.

The Ottoman Turk found his first opportunity to make capital of the Caliphate in the Treaty of Kuchuk Kainarji, in 1774, between Abdul Hamid I and Catherine II of Russia, under which treaty the Sultan surrendered all claim to the Tatars in southern Russia, that is to say in the Crimea and in the Kuban Steppes. Following the analogy of Catherine II, who claimed to be protectress of Orthodox Christians in Turkish territory, the Sultan's diplomats made a similar claim in regard to Moslems in Christian Russia. The Russians quickly recognized that such a clause would divide the loyalty of the Tatars and in 1783 struck the clause from the Treaty.

An error once set going is difficult to eradicate from popular opinion and belief and from the publications of historians. Jacques de Vitry, Bishop of Acre from 1216 to 1226, was one of the earliest to mislead Christendom, in saying that the Caliph was Pope of the Saracens. He was followed in this view by Matthew Paris, Marco Polo, and many Moslem writers. In fact, the view which came to be held thus in Christendom had a distinct reaction upon Turkish ideas and claims, with no foundation in Moslem writ or tradition, now maintained as *bona fide* by Turkish writers. Sultan Abdul Hamid II inserted in the Constitution set forth on December 24,

[1] This paragraph seems to misrepresent the Ottoman use of the title of Caliph. See Encycl. of Islam—articles *Khalifa* and *Selim I*, which both state that Selim used the title before his conquest of Egypt—[Samuel M. Zwemer, Ed. of *The Moslem World*].

1876, Article 3: "The Sublime Ottoman Sultanate, which possesses the Supreme Islamic Caliphate, will appertain to the eldest of the descendants of the house." Article 4: "H. M. the Sultan, as Caliph, is protector of the Moslem religion."

Consequent upon the disastrous wars in which Serbia, Rumania, and Montenegro gained complete independence, and as a result of which Bulgaria became a separate state under Turkish suzerainty, with Bosnia and Herzegovina ceded to Austria by the Treaty of Berlin, Abdul Hamid made a bid for sympathy on the strength of the claim of the Caliphate to such Asiatic Moslem governments as India, Afghanistan, Java, China, Egypt, and Tunis. The response was not forthcoming. His plea was met by the orthodox Sunni doctrine that the Caliph must be from the tribe of the Quraysh, from which no Turkish Sultan ever came. Even in Turkey there was opposition, and in 1890 Abdul Hamid ordered the tablets defining the qualifications of the Caliphate removed from the mosques.

In postwar Turkey, the idea took root that the Caliphate and its associations were not compatible with modern constitutional government, and on November 1, 1922, the Grand National Assembly declared the Sultanate at an end, and the republic established. Sultan Wahid-ud-Din was deposed and Abdul Majid was elected Caliph of all Moslems by the Grand National Assembly at Angora. He held an anomalous position until the Caliphate was finally abolished by the Angora government in March, 1924, when Abdul Majid was taken into exile by a British war vessel bound for Malta, whence he later joined King Hussein at Mecca.

The ex-Sultan, Wahid-ud-Din, has not been inactive, but has busied himself with various plots against the Nationalist regime. Secret service men of the Angora government recently accused him of being implicated in the late uprising in Kurdistan, with four aims in mind: his own restoration as Sultan, the reestablishment of the Ottoman Caliphate, the autonomy of Kurdistan, and the return of the seat of government to Constantinople.

But even today [in 1931] there are several claimants for the Caliphate. The late King of the Hijaz, Hussein, can well claim that he is a descendant of the tribe of Quraysh, an ancestry which would go a long way toward satisfying the Moslem legitimist. The Sharif of

Morocco is considered the Caliph by his people; several potentates in the Malay Archipelago put forward the claim; a Javanese Sultan, three chieftains of Borneo, the Sultan of Tidore in the Molucca Islands, a chief in Sumatra—all claim to be the Caliph of Islâm.

The Moslem ideal of a single Caliph who shall rule an ideal state, in which Mohammedan law shall govern every concern of life, will remain alive and will continue to be a rallying cry for faithful enthusiasts and Moslem or anti-Moslem propagandists. The idea of Pan-Islam appeals to Moslems as a reaction against foreign domination. But one ecumenical Caliph to rule over a unified Mohammedan culture and religion has never been a reality.

7

THE RISE OF ISLAMIC PHILOSOPHY

Richard Walzer

Greek philosophy is not found in Arabic dress before the first half of the ninth century, during the Caliphate of the Abbasids. The Abbasids had transferred the capital of the Muslim empire from Damascus to the newly founded city of Baghdād, and it was there that the two Islamic philosophers with whom I propose here to deal spent the greater part of their lives, Ya'qūb son of Isḥāq al-Kindī and Abū Naṣr al-Fārābī. The former of these, who died shortly after A.D. 870, witnessed the reign of the great Caliphs al-Ma'mūn (813-33) and al-Mu'taṣim (833-42), a period marked both by the power of the Abbasid Caliphate in the realm of politics, which was then at its height, and by a vigorous artistic and intellectual life. He was thus an older contemporary of the Greek patriarch Photius, who once came as an ambassador to the border of the Muslim Empire, and of the Irish philosopher Eriugena (John the Scot), who was the first to introduce Neoplatonic thought into the far west. The schoolmen were acquainted with al-Kindī's name, and knew a few of his treatises. Al-Fārābī, who was born about the time of al-Kindī's death, and died about A.D. 950, was of Turkish origin like the body guard of the Caliphs from al-Mu'taṣim onwards; he, too, was known to the Latin Middle Ages, under the name of AlFarabius, and was used, for example, by Gundisalvi. We see thus that both he and al-Kindī were

Reprinted, by permission, from *Oriens,* III (1950), 1-19. Footnotes have been omitted.

considerably earlier than Avicenna (980-1037) and Averroes (1126-98), who were the two Arabic philosophers most widely known in the West, and who are, for instance, found mentioned, along with the philosophers of ancient Greece, in the *Divina Commedia*; they stand as representatives of two contrasted types of Islamic philosophy, and so far as we know they were the first to establish them both.

To speak of "Islamic philosophy" may seem at first a contradiction in terms; philosophy was at home in ancient Greece, bound by close ties with the Greek way of life and with Greek religion, but Islam is a faith set in the Judaeo-Christian mold, based on a sacred book, the Qur'ān, which is invested with a divine authority no product of the Greek tradition ever enjoyed and determines in virtue of this the belief and conduct of every Muslim. It takes its stand entirely on divine revelation, and a Muslim's convictions are convictions of faith, whereas the philosophers of Greece, with a few rare exceptions to be mentioned later, consistently maintained the primacy of reason.

Nevertheless it was not in al-Kindī and al-Fārābī that the Greek tradition and the Hebraic, natural theology and sacred scriptures, met for the first time, though the earliest attempt to reconcile the two, made in the so-called Hellenistic period of Jewish culture, had ended in eventual failure when the Old Testament and the Law returned once more to an exclusive domination of Jewish life after the destruction of Jerusalem in A.D. 70 and the suppression of the revolt under Hadrian. The clash between Greek thought and Christian, on the other hand, led to a permanent connection between the two, rendered all the easier by the predominance of metaphysical and transcendental elements in the philosophy of Plotinus and his successors. In this case, unlike that of the Jews and of the Arabs, no linguistic difficulty was involved, the Old Testament being studied in the Septuagint version which Judaism had in the end rejected; while on the other hand Christianity had this in common with Mohammedanism, that they were both universal religions recognizing no national boundaries.

This naturalization of Greek thought within the Christian Church took two forms which it is important for us to note if we are to understand the background of Islamic theology (the so-called *kalām*) and philosophy. The first of these is the patristic theology which took its definite shape in the fourth century in the works of such men as St. Basil and Gregory Nazianzen in the East or St. Augustine in the West, borrowing mainly from the Platonic and Stoic schools and seeking to make the faith rationally intelligible without undermining its supernatural character; its motto was, in the words used later by St. Anselm, *credo ut intelligam.* The second, not less important, was the reception of the philosophical syllabus as found in the schools of Athens, Constantinople, Antioch and Alexandria, a tradition which lasted without a break from the time of Aristotle to the Muslim conquests, and on further through the first two centuries of Muslim rule. This reception, which took place about the middle of the fifth century, was at the time of the Muslim invasions an accomplished fact in the two Syriac churches, the Nestorian and the Jacobite, as well as in the Greek; at this period the philosophical syllabus comprised the lecture courses or treatises of Aristotle, expounded by commentators from the second century onwards, selected works of Plato (the selection differing in different schools), and the metaphysics of Neoplatonism, this again studied in different writers according to the preference of individual teachers. It is one of the distinctive features of Islamic philosophy, as represented in al-Kindī and al-Fārābī, Avicenna and Averroes, that it faced the problems which the impact of this Aristotelian and Neoplatonic tradition implied, and worked them out more thoroughly and consistently than did either their predecessors or their contemporaries in the Greek Church.

I shall now draw these introductory remarks to a close by seeking to justify the attempt to delineate Islamic philosophy in the period of its rise. That it became part of the tradition of the West was due mainly to the extensive translation of works of Avicenna and Averroes, men who were not, as were al-Fārābī and al-Kindī, the originators of the new movement in philosophy and religion, and so medievalists have been mainly interested in these later thinkers as providing the immediate Arabic background of medieval philosophy. They have been less interested in the process which made Avicenna and Averroes possible, in their Islamic affiliations and the manner in which they drew upon that phase of ancient philosophy which immediately preceded the rise of Islamic. But Islamic philosophy, apart from its claim to be understood on its own account, deserves consideration as part of the legacy of Greece, as an important link in that chain of civilization which comes to us from Hellenic antiquity. It was the uninterrupted study of Greek philosophy which guaranteed the continuity of that chain; Homer and Aeschylus were of minor importance, at least outside the evernarrowing boundaries of the Byzantine Empire, whereas Greek philosophy never died out; at the time when interest in it was low in the Latin West, it was intensively studied in the Islamic world and adapted there to a new setting.

I

Ya'qūb son of Isḥāq al-Kindī, who first introduced this Aristotelian-Neoplatonic philosophy into the Islamic world, was an Arab of noble descent. He was born in the Mesopotamian city of Basra, whose life had been deeply influenced by Jundi Shāpur, a celebrated centre of Persian learning nearby which was a meeting-place of Hellenic, Persian and Indian influences. Al-Kindī's father held a high position as governor of Kūfa, the other early Arabian city of Mesopotamia, and the son was evidently appreciated as a philosopher at the court of Baghdād, for important works of his are addressed to the great Caliph al-Ma'mūn and his successor al-Mu'taṣim, the latter of whom appointed him tutor to one of his sons. The distinguished position he enjoyed is unique in the annals of Islamic philosophy, and can only be explained on the assumption that he shared the form of Mohammedan theology fostered and supported by the rulers he served. The Caliph, as the prophet's successor, was the leader of a theocratic way of life as well as the political ruler of a vast empire, and al-Kindī's princely protectors entertained very decided religious views which they enforced upon their subjects with all the means at the disposal of absolute rulers, identifying themselves with the so-called Mu'tazila, then a living force and not (what it later became) merely one sect among others. These Mu'tazilites were champions of a reasonable creed against anthropomorphism and literalism on the one hand, and of an essentially religious standpoint against scepticism and unbelief on the other, standing out therefore as rational theologians by contrast with the non-rational, fideist attitude of theological orthodoxy, which was in disgrace in al-Kindī's day.

The facts of his life and the titles of his numerous works (now mostly lost) have always led scholars to assume that al-Kindī shared the Mu'tazilite standpoint and set himself to work out a place for philosophy within its theological framework. Incidentally the Mu'tazila itself was deeply influenced by Greek ideas and Greek methods of argument. On this point the recent discovery in Istanbul of an important manuscript of al-Kindī has converted likelihood into a matter of certainty. And so in al-Kindī we find a balance unique in early Islam between an "advanced" theology, based on reasoned interpretation of revelation, and a philosophy which aimed at utilizing the totality of our obviously limited human faculties in the understanding of God, the universe and man himself. That in this task he drew on the Greek philosophical tradition, and showed a considerable measure of success in its assimilation although he was the first to make the attempt, is a fact that needs to be stressed, and in this connection it would be interesting to try to discover his immediate predecessors in the Syriac world and perhaps too in the Greek; one might hope in this way to contribute towards a future history of Greek influences on the Syriac church and on medieval Islam. But if our ultimate aim is a complete understanding of the status Greek philosophy held in these foreign surroundings, the immediate question on which we have to concentrate our attention is this: "What was it that al-Kindī had in view when he introduced philosophy into the theological framework of the Mu'tazila, and where did he draw the dividing-line between philosophy and theology?"

In attempting to answer this question I shall draw upon three of his works, the first a short introduction to Aristotle surveying the contents of his treatises or, more probably, of summaries from them. The second, addressed to the Caliph al-Mu'taṣim, is entitled *First Philosophy* or *Metaphysics,* and demonstrates the existence of God in a Neoplatonic fashion, opening with a remarkable preface which explains the principles on which the treatise is based. Only the first half of this work has come down to us, Part II, in which he arrived at the same conclusions from a Mu'tazilite interpretation of the Qur'ān, having apparently disappeared; but the loss of this is compensated by the existence of another work, an Epistle addressed to the son of al-Mu'taṣim whose tutor he was. Here he pointed out that a verse of the Qur'ān asserting that the stars worship God was in full accord with the Neoplatonic form of Greek astral theology, Greek metaphysics since the time of Plato and Aristotle having based itself on the regular and unchanging revolution of the heavenly bodies and the divine nature which this indicated in them.

The first of these three treatises, that on Aristotle, shows us at once what is new in al-Kindī if only we compare it with the philosophy of ancient Greece. He gives a survey of the normal Aristotelian syllabus of a Neoplatonic school of the Athenian type, such as may well have been in use in the first half of the fifth century and so taken over by Nestorian Christian philosophers or theologians, from Antioch for example, driven by the Greek emperor to find refuge in some Persian centre. But, rather surprisingly at first sight, he includes in this survey a long excursus on the difference between human knowledge and divine, between the toilsome enquiries of the philosopher and the intuitive insight of the prophet. "Ordinary mankind" he says, "are by nature incapable of such knowledge, all matters of this type being beyond their capacities and efforts; all they can do is submit with docile obedience, professing faith in the revelations of the prophets."

In many cases, according to al-Kindī, philosophy and revelation arrive at the same result, though in different ways, but there are certain fundamental tenets of faith which are not rationally demonstrable and are guaranteed by scripture, prophecy, and revealed religion alone; in the section just quoted he discusses two, common to Christianity and Islam, which presented all but insuperable difficulties to the Greek mind—the resurrection of the body on the Day of Judgment and the creation of the world from nothing in a single moment of time by the omnipotent will of God. That the world should come from nothing was irreconcilable with a constantly repeated axiom of Greek thought, and could be demonstrated by Scripture alone, by the word of God himself as found in the Qur'ān. Greek philosophy had attempted rational demonstration of the immortality of man's soul, a doctrine maintained by Plato and the Neoplatonists and, in his earlier years, by Aristotle, but the resurrection of the dead in bodily form was never considered by the philosophers of Greece as even a remote possibility; it was a conception utterly inconceivable to the Greek philosophical mind. It could thus be accepted as a miracle alone, as expounded in the thirty-sixth Sura of the Qur'ān, to which al-Kindī refers as a particularly striking example of prophetic inspiration. This Qur'ānic saying al-Kindī could interpret in the same manner as the Mu'tazilites, amplifying it with philosophical arguments which lent it an added probability, but he made no attempt to give a stringent demonstration of the creation of the world from nothing and the resurrection of the flesh.

Here, however, we have an extreme case, and it is only when fundamental issues of this character are involved that al-Kindī appears as a theologian of the type of St. Basil—or, as he would perhaps put it, whenever revelation unlocked the door to a domain of reality to which Greek philosophy had not provided the key. Elsewhere, as for example in his *Metaphysics* and in the commentary on the passage of the Qur'ān (mentioned above) in which the stars are said to worship God, he adheres unconditionally to the scheme of the universe which had been constructed by Aristotle and subsequently completed by the Neoplatonic theory of emanation from the Divine Being, and to which, with all its beauty and imposing consistency, there was nothing comparable in the Islamic tradition.

He had, however, to change it in a small but not unimportant detail. The highest sphere of the heavens, that which comes next after God, who is the first cause of the universe as its unmoved mover and the inexhaustible source of emanation, is the proximate cause of life in the sublunar world, i.e., on the earth. But the universe was, on the view of Aristotle and the Neoplatonists, eternal and uncreated, and, if al-Kindī's aim was to harmonize philosophy with Islamic theology as the Mu'tazilites understood it, he needed to transform this latter in a small though important detail. He may have had a Christian predecessor here, but if so the fact in no way affects the result. The highest sphere of the heavens, according to al-Kindī, having once been created from nothing by God, will last as long as God so wills; it is obedient to God's decree, and on it the other regions of the world depend, as the philosophers have explained. Once it perishes, the remainder of the universe will perish too, since the divine energy will no longer be transmitted to the lower strata.

Within these limits, therefore, philosophy helps towards a more adequate understanding of reality, but it never in al-Kindī contradicts the established theology of his day; for him, therefore, philosophy is the handmaid of theology and of divine revelation, nowhere claiming a predominance over the latter. Al-Fārābī on the contrary, as we shall see, represents an attitude diametrically opposed; first and foremost a philosopher, he stresses the primacy of reason over the symbolic expressions of revealed religion. But al-Kindī's description of the supreme being in purely negative terms is in full agreement with the mode in which the Mu'tazilites speak of Him, and so he makes no claim to achieve by means of Greek philosophy anything beyond what the traditionalists and Mu'tazilites had previously attempted, viz., a profounder understanding of the fundamental principles of the Muslim faith. He does, however, claim, not without justification, that his new approach is superior to anything tried before, and having once been introduced will henceforward be indispensable.

In the preface to his *Metaphysics* al-Kindī explains why he needs to have recourse to Greek philosophy, though it is of foreign origin and no part of Muhammad's revelation. In view of the brevity of human life one cannot afford to neglect the achievements of previous thinkers simply because they were of a different race and creed. "We should not, then, be ashamed to recognize truth and assimilate it, from whatever quarter it may reach us, even though it may come from earlier generations and foreign peoples. For the seeker after truth is nothing of more value than truth itself; it never cheapens or debases the seeker, but ennobles and elevates him." Philosophy seems thus to amount simply to a gradual accumulation of truths already accepted, to which later generations can hope to do no more than provide minor corrections and additions. But, as we have already seen, al-Kindī is at the same time aware that every fresh thinker who sifts the accumulated store of truth may see it in a new light and approach it with new questions in his mind arising out of his own experience of life. He expresses himself thus: "We must, then, remain faithful to the principle we have followed in all our works, which is first to quote in full what the ancients have said on any subject and then to fill in what they have not fully expressed, and this according to the usage of the Arabic language, the customs of our age, and our individual ability." It was this attitude of mind which made him not an epigonus of later Greek philosophy but the first philosopher of Islam, the philosopher of the Mu'tazilite theology, convinced that faith and reason, theology and philosophy, were to be synthesized, the latter confirming the tenets of faith and deepening the world-view transmitted to us by the intuitive insight of the prophets.

Against orthodox literalism he urges that, while the prophet has an apostolic mission and the truth of his message is indisputable, once the prospect of philosophy has been opened before them men are bound to philosophize and cannot shirk the issue. This argument comes from the lost *Protrepticus* of Aristotle, a work imitated in the *Hortensius* of Cicero, which deeply influenced the religious development of St. Augustine; it was an argument employed in similar circumstances by Clement of Alexandria in the second century A.D. "They must declare the attainment of philosophical knowledge either necessary or unnecessary; if they say it is necessary, they must agree to go in search of it; if not necessary, they must offer reasons and arguments to prove their assertion. But to give reasons and arguments involves one in the attainment of philosophical knowledge in its essential truth, and hence the attainment of philosophical knowledge is necessary and obligatory for them also."

It is scarcely surprising that we are indebted to al-Kindī, as to many other Arabic philosophers, for new material for the history of Greek philosophy. The arguments he uses are not always to be traced in such Neoplatonic works as we possess in the original Greek, and so add to our knowledge of Neoplatonism, and treatises on the soul on Neoplatonic lines have yielded two new fragments of a lost dialogue of Aristotle, the *Eudemus,* written at the period when he still adhered to Plato's theory of the immortality of the soul. He arranged for a translation, for the benefit of his royal pupil, of the so-called *Theology of Aristotle,* which, going back ultimately to some highly competent paraphrase of the philosophical essays of Plotinus, represents the only remnant we possess of an ancient commentary on him and deserves to be much better appreciated by his readers.

To ask for al-Kindī's sources is certainly legitimate, for he always insists that the substance of his arguments is Greek and that he has only changed them when specifically Islamic issues are involved. His philosophy was based on Aristotelianism as developed by the Neoplatonists, who stressed the Platonic element in the Platonic-Aristotelian tradition and were particularly concerned to prove how God governed the world as its First Cause and guaranteed its existence. But we should like to know further whether al-Kindī can be connected with any particular Neoplatonic school, for, though they may appear more or less alike from a distance, they had, it is recognized, individual features of their own. Conclusions must be provisional until all the available evidence has been closely examined, but the examination of small details appears to point to one particular quarter as that which influenced al-Kindī, one to which more general considerations would themselves incline the enquirer to turn.

The school in question is the Neoplatonic of the first half of the fifth century, which had taken on a specific coloring under the influence of Iamblichus, the contemporary of Constantine the Great; here alone in the history of Greek speculation were philosophy and theology studied side by side, theology (based on such revelations as those of the Chaldaean oracles) demanding unconditional belief from its adherents, and philosophy being regarded as no more than a substructure for it. In the present state of research it appears probable that Nestorian philosophers from Antioch, deriving from a Neoplatonic tradition close to the Athenian pattern, carried it with them when they were expelled from the Byzantine empire and found refuge in Persia. This later system—a bizarre one to the eyes of the classical scholar—they may have adapted to their own needs by substituting the Old and New Testaments for the outlandish authorities of the Neoplatonists, while maintaining the same relations between faith and reason as their predecessors. Al-Kindī in his turn may then be thought of as having substituted Muhammad and the Qur'ān for St. Paul and the Bible, adhering in other respects to the Neoplatonic scheme, which may have undergone some decline or, at any rate, simplification during the three centuries which elapsed between the end of the Athenian school and the foundation of the Abbasid empire.

II

The pattern of al-Kindī's philosophy, welcome as it might appear to a Muslim mind such as that of al-Ghazālī, is very unusual in

Greek thought. But what is it that happens when a Muslim philosopher tries to naturalize, within an Islamic civilization, a philosophy of the Greek pattern, which is more familiar to us? This is the first new feature which we notice in al-Fārābī, the feature which distinguishes him sharply from his predecessor, producing a very different set of relationships between religion and philosophy and one more closely akin to that suggested by the title of a lost work of Strato, *On the Royal Position of Philosophy,* Περὶ βασιλείας φιλοσοφίας. To understand al-Fārābī's background let us consider for a moment this type of philosophy, which is that represented by Plato, Aristotle and the Stoics. Here there is no revelation to be held in awe; philosophy molds the tradition, refining and reshaping it constantly, itself the highest and most spiritual form of Greek religion once we mark off the religion of the mind from the customary observance of public worship. In Plato we have a religious genius and a great philosopher in one, and, whether accepted, modified or rejected he dominates the whole future history of philosophy. In a philosophical system of this kind traditional religion is valued either for utilitarian reasons or as providing a symbolical approach to a truth which can be properly grasped by the mind of the philosopher alone, and so Plato and others after him set their hand to schemes of education and legislation on a large scale, trying to mold the lives of the non-philosophers in accordance with the philosophical insight they had attained. Plato in his old age dealt in the *Phaedrus* with rhetoric as the art of conveying philosophical truth to unphilosophical minds, and made in the *Laws* his most elaborate attempt to lay down a code of behavior and formulate the institutions of an ethical society based on the new religion of the mind which he had constructed; he was by no means satisfied with having simply established the inner freedom and independence of the individual philosopher and his claim to rule the state.

This aspect of Platonism survived the breakdown of the Greek city-state, and we meet it again in, for instance, the *De Republica* of Cicero or in Eusebius' *Outline of the Duties of a Christian Emperor.* We have every reason for thinking that it was also transmitted through the Greek schools down to the establishment of Islamic civilization, though rejected by Plotinus and the Neoplatonic school of Athens, who emphasized and refined upon the transcendental and mystical side of Plato. Recent discoveries of hitherto unknown texts of al-Fārābī have proved that it was from this interpretation of Plato that he started openly; the kind of philosophy he aimed at establishing was not based simply on the primacy of reason, but included also the Platonic view that it was the duty of the philosopher to give traditional religion its proper place in an ideal state, fashioning it according to his philosophical insight, and likewise, being himself perfect in every respect, to lay claim to the rule of the state, whether it be a city-state or cover the whole Islamic world or even the whole inhabited part of the earth.

That in this he was inspired by Plato is evident; this Greek tradition had reached the Muslim world before al-Fārābī's day, and by the time of his birth there existed complete Arabic translations or summaries not only of the *Timaeus,* which was held in esteem in the Western world too, but also of the *Republic* and *Laws,* which remained there completely unknown. His immediate teachers were not Nestorian Christians, as were al-Kindī's but Jacobites, tracing back their descent to the Neoplatonic school of Alexandria, not to that of Athens.

But this different attitude which we find in al-Fārābī to the relations between philosophy and religion, and similarly his interest in the ideal ruler, had their roots in genuine Islamic problems as well, and it may have been they which opened his eyes to the type of philosophy just mentioned. The question who was the legitimate heir of the prophet, as at the same time the political leader and the religious, had been a burning one in the Islamic world from the very beginning without ever being finally settled. Al-Kindī had lived at the zenith of the Abbasid Caliphate, in an atmosphere markedly favorable to his philosophical activities and under rulers who not merely tolerated but actively supported the influx of Greek philosophy and science. But since then there had been a change; the Mu'tazilite theologians were now considered a dangerous element, already in al-Kindī's old age the philosophers had fallen into disgrace under the caliphate of al-Mutawakkil (847-61), and now and in al-Fārābī's day the Caliphs, identifying themselves with a strictly orthodox interpretation of Islam, viewed philosophy with mistrust. Al-Fārābī was a younger contemporary of al-Ash'arī, the founder of orthodox Muslim theology, and lived at the time of the steady decline of the Abbasids. It is this state of affairs which lies behind a statement, made apparently in a completely detached and objective manner, to be found in his last work, that on the ideal state: "If at a given time it should happen that wisdom (i.e., philosophy) has no share in the government, though every other qualification for rule may be present, the ideal state will remain rulerless, the actual head of the state will be no true king, and the state will head for destruction; and if no wise man is to be found and associated with the acting head of the state, then after a certain interval the state will undoubtedly perish." It is worthy of notice that Plato had made the same challenge to Athens during the decline of the Greek city-state, and that Cicero had renewed the demand for a philosopher-ruler during the supreme crisis of the Roman republic; it is in periods when the established political forms are in decay that Plato's view has again and again been put forward.

Al-Fārābī did not belong to the ruling class. A poor man, he had few material needs and lived the life of an ascetic. He makes it clear that he had to hide his views so far as they concerned the religious questions of his day, but nevertheless he did not choose to express himself in allegorical or otherwise enigmatic language. His intention is that we shall understand his philosophical treatises as they stand, guessing their application for ourselves, but he is very sparing in his hints and thus it is often difficult to understand the way in which he wished his writing and teaching to influence the Islamic world; it was not for him to express his allegiance to definite political or religious groups as openly as had al-Kindī. Eventually he left Baghdad, whether of his own accord or under compulsion, and passed the last years of his life at the court of a famous ruler of Aleppo, Saif ad-Daula, who was in his politics and on the question of the true Caliph an opponent of the prophet's recognized successor.

We must try first to understand how al-Fārābī, in a manner very different from that of al-Kindī, tried to assign to philosophy a dominating position in the Islamic world, doing so without hostility to Islam and without ceasing to be a devout Muslim himself. Like al-Kindī he believed that philosophy alone would enable Islam to reach its perfection and fulfil its highest destiny, but his formula turns out to be quite new, and as original in its way as that advocated by his predecessor.

At the end of his *De Beatitudine Assequenda* al-Fārābī makes the following pronouncement: "Philosophy has come down to us from the Greeks, from Plato and Aristotle, both of whom have given us not merely the results of their meditations but also the processes which led to them and the way to revive philosophy whenever it has become deficient, or has fallen out of existence." He does not, like his predecessor, claim simply to be following the Greeks; he goes on to assert that Greek philosophy is in complete decay in its native home and that he himself is about to revive it in the Islamic world. It had indeed, he claims elsewhere, had its ultimate origin among the Chaldaeans, at the centre of the Abbasid empire of his day, whence it passed to Egypt, to be handed down from the Egyptians to the Greeks, who were the first to produce a written philosophy; from the Greeks it passed to the Syrians and thence to the Arabs, and thus, after a long exile, it has returned to its native land, to be restored there to its former glory by al-Fārābī and others like him.

Plato and Aristotle were the authorities he followed, and, like the ancients from Cicero and Porphyry onwards, he believed in the ultimate identity of their views. But the way in which he reconciled them was a peculiar one, not to be traced in our extant Greek sources. He followed Aristotle in logic, natural science, psychology, metaphysics, and ethics, metaphysics being taken and developed on Neoplatonic lines, just as we have observed in the case of al-Kindī, and approximating to the account of God given by the Mu'tazilites. His comprehension of Aristotle was deeper and subtler than al-Kindī's—he could rely on better texts, due primarily to Ḥunain ibn Isḥāq and his pupils, who had produced, since al-Kindī's day, the best translations of Greek philosophy into Arabic. His own teachers, too, may have given him a greater familiarity with the Greek commentators on Aristotle, whether Neoplatonic or earlier. Al-Fārābī was, indeed, known to later Muslim philosophers as the second teacher—second, that is, to Aristotle, whose follower he was in both theoretical philosophy and moral. In political theory, however, he was not a disciple of Aristotle, whose *Politics* was very little studied in the late Greek schools (we have no Greek commentary on it, nor any early Byzantine manuscript, as we have of the other lecture-courses of Aristotle). For he substitutes Plato's *Republic* and *Laws*, convinced that Plato's theoretical speculations have been superseded by Aristotle and the Neoplatonists but clinging to Plato's solution of the problems of politics.

In virtue of this he occupies a unique position; Plato's ideal state enjoyed no great measure of popularity in the Neoplatonic school of Athens, nor consequently in the Platonic schools of the Italian Renaissance, dependent as these were on that interpretation of Plato as it reached them through Byzantium. The *Republic* was not, so far as I know, studied much in the early Christian Church or among the Fathers; nor was it translated into Latin when, through the version made by William of Moerbeke from the Greek, the schoolmen became acquainted with Aristotle's *Politics*. Averroes, who in this and other respects followed al-Fārābī, wrote a paraphrase of the *Republic* which is preserved in a Hebrew translation and in a Latin (the latter, however, not made in the thirteenth century from the Arabic, as were many other translations of Averroes' commentaries, but as late as the sixteenth century and from the Hebrew). It is doubtful whether this particular harmonization of Plato and Aristotle is al-Fārābī's own work, or due to some Greek systematization, now lost, which appealed to him; myself I incline to the latter alternative.

This attitude of al-Fārābī's led him to assert the primacy of philosophy over religion, and therewith to attempt to reshape, or at any rate reorganize, the whole Islamic tradition from the point of view of his philosophy. If the Caliph—the Imām, as he calls him—is to be philosopher-ruler or philosopher-legislator, then every aspect of Islamic life must be affected by this introduction of the new Greek ideas and so put on a new basis. The philosopher can now no longer be satisfied with merely providing, as al-Kindī appears to have done, a purely intellectual substructure for the subject matter of theology; he will attempt the application to Islam of that three fold division of theology, originating with the Stoics and found mentioned in such writers as St. Augustine, according to which there are three theologies, the mythical, the legal and the natural, propounded respectively by poets, legislators, and philosophers. In Greece the poets would be represented by Homer, allegorically interpreted as by the Stoics or subjected to philosophical modifications as in Plato's *Republic* and Laws (it has indeed, not without reason, been suggested that Dante would be the ideal poet for meeting Plato's requirements). This place al-Fārābī assigns to the Qur'ān; in a Christian *milieu,* such as he and his disciples seem also to have had in mind, it would be occupied by the Old and New Testaments. Political theology included the official state religion, with its forms of worship, institutions and religious and civil laws, such a scheme as was outlined for instance in the *Laws* of Plato, and for it al-Fārābī substituted the Sharī'a, the divinely ordained Mohammedan law, the "highway of divine commandments and instruction." This was an obvious substitution for the Greek system of religious and civil law for a philosopher living in an Arabic-speaking Muslim society, and not in a Greek city-state or the Eastern Roman Empire. But he seems to have considered advising his philosopher-legislator or Imām to imbue the Islamic Sharī'a with Greek tradition, not the details but the legal principles as they are found in Plato's *Laws.* The Qur'ān and the Sharaī'a, or in other words the mythical and the political theology, which make up the religion of Islam, convey truth in symbolical form only, according to the view al-Fārābī derived from his Greek predecessors. This may be conveniently illustrated by his attitude to the resurrection of the flesh, an essential tenet of the faith unconditionally accepted by al-Kindī. For al-Fārābī, as for a Stoic for instance, the assertion of the resurrection of the dead is valid only in the sphere of religion, where forms of expression are employed differing from those of philosophical demonstration; stories of rewards and punishments in a future life have value only symbolically and as serving to improve the conduct of the ordinary man. This, according to al-Fārābī, must have been what Muhammad intended when he introduced this doctrine into the Qur'ān. Speaking as a philosopher he rejects the resurrection of the flesh; like Cicero in the *Somnium Scipionis,* he allows the resurrection of good souls alone, and he does not, like Plato and the youthful Aristotle, believe in transmigration. From this it follows that al-Fārābī could not accord the Mu'tazilite or any other rational theology the same esteem as did al-Kindī, who placed it above philosophy (theology being, on al-Kindī's view, grounded in the indubitable certainty of divine revelation). For al-Fārābī the highest position belongs to metaphysics, and theology (*kalām*) can occupy no more than the second place, that corresponding to Aristotle's dialectic as found in the *Topics*—starting from views generally accepted but not capable of serving as the premises of strictly scientific demonstration according to the rules enunciated in the *Posterior Analytics*.

The truths of philosophy can be understood and grasped by philosophers of all religions and races; they are the same for all, but the individual philosopher shares a particular religion and a particular Sharī'a; he is a human being, and as such he cannot live exclusively in the realm of abstract thought: to do so would make him equal to God, who is pure mind. An Islamic philosopher is educated in Islamic customs and taught the Qur'ān before he can begin to philosophize, and remains a Muslim the whole of his life, and the same would apply to a Christian philosopher in his attitude to his native religion. Hence it was that al-Fārābī could have Christian teachers in philosophy—not merely Christian assistance in the way of translations from Greek or Syriac philosophical texts—and could have Christians as well as Muslims among his disciples. The ideal Muslim philosopher will thus be trained in a way similar to Plato's philosopher-king, to whose education al-Fārābī specifically refers, with the gymnastic side tacitly omitted, and it is he who should rule the Muslim community as Imām and successor of the prophet. How this is to be brought about we are nowhere told—presumably by divine appointment (*θεία τύχη*), as Plato puts it. This philosopher-king may rule the whole inhabited world, giving to all established religions their due position and equal rights; but if this is impossible he will rule the Islamic world alone, and the development will in any case start in Islamic lands, since philosophy, according to al-Fārābī, is now dead in Greece but may be revived on Muslim soil in its old home of 'Irāq.

As in Plato, metaphysics and politics are intimately connected in al-Fārābī's scheme for an ideal state. The same order prevails in the universe, in man and in the ideal state, and just as the divine mind rules the universe and guarantees its existence, so the mind ought to govern the soul of man and organize society in the most perfect manner. This is what we find in Plato's *Gorgias, Republic,* and *Timaeus,* as well as in Neopythagorean imitations of Plato and in al-Fārābī; the universe, the individual man and the state cannot be considered in isolation, and once the philosopher becomes the supreme ruler all the more detailed problems of society can be solved. It is essential, however, that he shall first have molded his own soul after the right pattern.

Al-Fārābī's perfect man or perfect philosopher will not be without the intuitive gifts of prophecy, but as in Plato they will be subordinated to his philosophical powers, instead of predominating as they do in the Athenian Neoplatonism in and after the time of Proclus. It is undeniable that his view is quite incompatible with Islam in its established form.

It is not surprising that al-Fārābī, too, provides us with new materials for the history of Greek philosophy; in his case they serve less for the transcendental aspects of that philosophy than for what we may call the political interpretation of Plato, neglected in the school of Iamblichus and his successors. We may, indeed, recover from him a whole Platonic system, together with an account of the dialogues on these lines and summaries of the *Laws* and the *Republic.* We have here a welcome confirmation for those recent students of Plato who have insisted that equal consideration requires to be bestowed on the metaphysical side of his work, on the ethical and on the political.

8

LITERARY TENDENCIES

Francesco Gabrieli

By "Islâm" [we mean] . . . here the whole "Muslim civilization" which developed, with its own physiognomy, from Central Asia to the Atlantic, in faith in Mohammed's message and in the wake of the Arab diaspora. Chronologically this civilization appeared in the seventh century and lasted until, ceasing to be autonomous after having ceased to be fruitful, it entered a crisis and was transformed, at the touch of the West, at about the end of the eighteenth century. Religious faith unquestionably furnished to this civilization not only its common denominator but also its axis and fundamental aspect. All other aspects of life—material and spiritual, political and literary, economic and social—bear this religious element's mark, take color from its reflections, and develop under its influence. Islâm, it has been said, is more than any other a totalitarian religion, and it encompasses the whole man, not his religious consciousness alone.

While holding strictly to these premises, it is legitimate, however, to seek to distinguish the other factors making up the historical picture of Muslim civilization, along with the religious factor that influenced them. We want to speak of the literary factor here, not as a purely aesthetic element—which would lead to a study of distinctive personalities standing out against the background of a tra-

Reprinted from *Unity and Variety in Muslim Civilization,* ed. Gustave E. von Grunebaum, by permission of the University of Chicago Press. Discussion and notes have been omitted.

dition—but as the study of the tradition itself or, rather, of the several changing and contrasted traditions that reflect the antinomy, "unity and variety of Islâm," in the literary field. Such an antinomy forces itself on anyone who comes into contact with this civilization: behind the rigorously uniform façade of religion, law, and social custom, we can guess, and now and then perceive, that multiplicity conditioned in space and time that gives us the concrete reality within the abstract schema—the live organism behind the stylized expression of the statue. Of course it is a very hard and delicate thing to grasp this life and the secret reality which is masked under the smooth uniformity of the external facies. Where the literary field that occupies us here is concerned, the undertaking is exceedingly difficult and practically hopeless if we aim to come upon cases of "individuality" submerged in the tradition; it is easier, on the other hand, if we can limit ourselves, as we have set out to do, to bringing out the contrasts and varieties of the literary traditions as indexes of the variety within the fundamental unity of the civilization we are studying.

Limiting oneself to these contrasts of traditions also lessens an author's presumption when he extends his judgments to more than one literature, as anyone must do who wants to study this phenomenon, at least in principle, over the whole area of Muslim civilization. We have still another and perhaps better excuse in the fact that over this whole area a single language and a single literature, the Arabic, held predominance and absolute power for some time. Moreover, even where this language and literature lost their primacy in the course of time, their influence did not come to an end, at least within the chronological limits we have indicated. For this reason it is perhaps not so grievous for an Arabist to be speaking here about tendencies and contrasts "in Islâm," rather than an Iranist or a Turkologist, for the Arabic literary contribution is in the forefront of our picture by its proportions in space and time and by its intensity of tone and color; the Arabist speaking in general terms about Islâm might even—to his detriment, certainly, but without getting beyond his depth—somewhat neglect the other two master literatures of the Muslim world, but every informed person knows how inconceivable would be the contrary procedure. Thus Arabic literature (or, better, literature "in Arabic") figures preeminently as our subject; and, next, Persian literature, which comes immediately after the Arabic in historical richness and importance but which equals it and perhaps surpasses it in artistic value. When we come to studies referring to the last leg of the "tripod," Turkish literature and its dependencies, both the competence of the present writer and the absolute and relative importance of the subject in the hierarchy of Muslim literatures decline.

Let us now look at this Arabic literature, which came into being, in an already fixed and stylized language, before Islâm itself, and which has furnished a common denominator to our studies. No one can fail to recognize the bonds existing between the literary heritage of pre-Islamic Persia and its later elaboration in the Muslim period; further, it is impossible not to notice the ties, albeit looser and more exceptional, between pre-Muslim Turkish literature, or rather folklore, and the Turks' first timid literary efforts inside Islâm. Neither the Persians nor the Turks, however, continued in the Muslim period to cultivate, except perhaps in certain forms of popular art, any literary products such as had existed in their pre-Islamic period; this is just what Muslim Arabic poetry did, on the contrary, borrowing its forms and its themes from pagan Arabic poetry over a period of centuries as from a model that for a long time seemed incomparable. Along with this poetry, the Sacred Book of Islâm, revealed in Arabic (*Qur'ânan 'arabiyyan*), the very Word of God which was afterwards felt to be uncreated, forever sanctified the religious and literary primacy of Arabic within Islâm. Arabic was subsequently spread as the language of the believers and conquerors, from the Jazîrat al-'Arab to the Mediterranean Basin and to Hither Asia. Less than a hundred years after the Prophet's death, it was the official, dominant, if not exclusive, language of government as well as of literature, and it was so from the banks of the Tagus to those of the Jaxartes; so true was this that verses were written in the same Arabic, according to the metrics, diction, and style of the oldest desert poets, at Cordova and at Kairouan, at Fusṭâṭ and at Damascus, at Kûfa, at Merv, and at Bukhara. The cultures that were old national possessions, or that previous history had transplanted into countries where Muslim conquest now extended, rapidly withered or even disappeared altogether before the new Arabo-Islamic culture, which, from the day it arose, conquered and absorbed all pre-existing elements. Latin, Greek, Coptic, Syriac, Armenian, and Pahlevi weakened and tended to disappear as living languages before Arabic's advance; and, when the Abbasids substituted their theocratic and supernational empire for the Arab national state, Arabic nevertheless remained the master language, used even by those who fought the cultural hegemony of the Arabs. The great Abbasid culture in Iraq, during the second and third centuries of the hegira (ninth and tenth centuries A.D.), which marked the apex of Arabo-Muslim intellectual effort, was at the same time the heart and the crucible of Arabic classical literature, which extended its influence from the extreme west to Transoxania. In these two centuries this literature created all its art forms, discussed its vital problems, was opened to the influence of prior great cultures, beginning with the Greek, and thus wrote the most brilliant page in medieval Islamic civilization. In the beginning of the eleventh century of our era, the heartbeats of Arab culture grew weaker in Iraq, only to stop altogether after the Mongol invasion, while the peripheral centers, which were Syria and Egypt, the Maghrib and Spain, burned with the brighter light. The fourteenth century, as is now commonly admitted, saw the end of Arabic literature as a creative force, after a life of at least seven centuries. Even more rapid in development, its younger sister in Persia had already had its finest classical period by the time of our Renaissance, while the Turkish Osmanli and Chaghatai literatures, the last to appear, began at just this period to live on the hand-me-downs of their two elder sisters—in the most artificial kind of hothouse existence, to the point of total captivation.

In this long and vast cycle of the pre-eminent Islamic literature, what distinctions, groupings, or contrasts can be brought out? The purely formal problem of a historical-scholarly division takes on new meaning if we consider it in the light of the criterion we have adopted here, that is, investigating variety in the literary field: a succession and a contrasting coexistence of tendencies within an apparently static civilization. It is obvious that divisions which are simply chronological or geographical (literature of east and west) cannot suffice, although they contain, in addition to their practical usefulness, undeniable elements of reality. It is necessary to integrate them into an *ab intus* analysis of the Arabic literary process.

Islâm at its origin found a national poetic tradition that was already stabilized and blossoming. The Prophet's own rather slight inclination and competence for poetry, and the traces of polemic which as a result remained in the Koran itself and in Tradition, did not prevent him from recognizing the social value which poetry had long had for the Arabs and from utilizing it for his ends. But although recent studies have weakened the old thesis of the total impermeability of the ancient poetry to the Islamic message, there remains nonetheless the fundamental fact of the contrast, analyzed masterfully by Goldziher, between *muruwwa* and *dîn*—between the pagan ideals, of which the antique poetry had become the vehicle, and Mohammed's Islamic ideal, which the first generations of Muslims developed. Islâm's totalitarian character, which we mentioned above, should logically have led to the condemnation of poetry as a frivolous and even impious foe of revelation, a living witness to vanquished paganism, a diabolic inspiration of the jinns. If this did not happen at all, and if poetry continued undisturbed on its way) with sporadic concessions to the new faith but keeping its themes, motifs, and images intact, as well as its power to fascinate even the minds of the pious), this was due not only to the art's "charm"—a charm that Plato recognized when he banished the art from his Republic—but also to the unbroken continuity among the first Muslim generations of a specific national awareness and pride which the new religion never succeeded in removing completely from their souls. The "Muslim" never succeeded in killing the "Arab" in these men, for whom poetry had constituted the sole means of expression, the sole affirmation of spirituality, and, according to the well-known definition, the record of his pageantry, the living memento of his past. Thus it was that the old poetry survived the *metanoia* of Islâm and was saved from oblivion, gathered into collections, and studied. It has been said that this was done because the ancient poetry contained documentary material for the exact understanding of the Holy Book, and this is partially true; but the whole archaic period of imitation of pre-Islamic poetry, which was pursued in the first century of Islâm and which was to constitute one of the poles of the "Ancients-Moderns" quarrel under the Abbasids, proves that this poetry was nevertheless experienced not only as a means but as an end, with an artistic and historic dignity of its own. The Ancients par excellence, the *mutaqaddimûn,* were the pagan poets, and the fact that two centuries after the end of the *jâhiliyya* they could still be considered by erudite Muslims as an unparalleled model to imitate reveals in our opinion not only a nearsighted classicism—a narrow, archaic, and scholastic notion of poetry—but also a tenacious and perhaps unconscious survival of what we might, "with a grain of salt," call the "humanism" of the *jâhiliyya*—a scale of values, a stylistic and poetic tradition which Islâm might well have been able to eject and which yet maintained itself with an astonishing vitality.

It was not accidental, indeed, that Goldziher, in his analysis of the motives which in the Abbasid period favored the appearance of the "new school" of the *muḥdathûn,* gave a leading place to an element which was neither literary nor ethnic but religious, that is, the growing devaluation of paganism and its ideals in favor of the Muslim *dîn*. But to be consistent, this reversal of values should have led to a revolt not against the antique poetry alone but against all poetry, admitting at most gnomic and ascetic versification of Abû al-'Atâhiya's type. The "Moderns" movement, on the contrary, seems to have been the most daring attempt to renovate the poetic themes and forms which the antique Arabic literature had known—a renovation which was, to be sure, inspired not by rigorist conceptions but by love of the art, by a more fully developed aesthetic awareness, by complex and delicate exigencies of a social kind. We wish to point out that the new literary currents of the Abbasid period and the polemics which they entailed, although abandoning the myth of the *jâhiliyya*—and in this agreeing with pietistic tendencies—did not, however, abandon but rather enlarged the humanistic ideal involved, brought over from the life-styles of pre-Islamic Arabia to the urban society of Iraq in the ninth and tenth centuries and to that of other urban centers in medieval Islâm. As a whole, the fundamental contrast, which nobody then dared explicitly to formulate but which we can today see more clearly, was not so much between "old and new poetry," between Ancients and Moderns, as between, let us repeat, *muruwwa* and *dîn,* between anthropocentric humanism and theocentric religiosity, between Arabic poetry and Muslim piety. Strictly speaking, indeed, the incomparable Revelation, with its *i'jâz* which was considered even formally perfect, should have depreciated and undermined every other effort at artistic expression; so true is this that a theologian and cultivated literary man of the tenth century, al-Bâquillânî, having undertaken to test Koranic *i'jâz* in style itself, submitted to equally close criticism an Ancient and a Modern poet, Imru'al-Qais, and al-Buḥturî. Happily for mankind, poetry never died out and resisted even the most hostile imputations, whether theological or philosophic, explicit or latent.

In purely literary terms, the struggle of the new Abbasid school to consolidate itself against the antique tradition undoubtedly constitutes the most interesting episode in the history of Arabic literature during its classical period. The weapons with which this battle was carried on and its progressive victory during the tenth century are the subjects of Goldziher's study cited above: from Ibn Qutaiba, who remained halfway between correct historical intuition ("No age has a monopoly of poetry; every ancient was modern in his time") and the crushing weight of tradition (forbidding the Moderns to adapt the canonical framework of the *qaṣîda* to the new conditions of life), all the way to the Maghribî school of al-Ḥuṣrî and Ibn Rashîq and to the gifted Ibn al-Athîr, we are able to follow a liberation of literary criticism from the classicist yoke, up to the affirmation of the superiority of the *muḥdathûn* over the venerated *fuḥûl* of antiquity. But to this victory in criticism there did not correspond any true and lasting victory in practice, which would have led to the total shattering of the consecrated frames. It has been noted that, in large part due to al-Mutanabbî's work (d. A.D. 965), a new classicism tainted with preciosity (the most questionable heritage of the "Moderns") weighed upon Arabic poetry after the tenth century and definitively ossified it. It had already been known to what straits this poetry was reduced, at least in the east, after the year 1000; and recent study on the poets of the lesser period now confirms this, as witness Rikâbî's study on the Ayyubid poets. For these, the artistic renovation and the critical labors of the great Abbasid period—the work of a Jâḥiẓ (d. 869) or an Ibn Qutaiba (d. 889), not to mention the isolated efforts of the Hellenist Qudâma (first half of tenth century)—had been in vain, and a saddening neoclassical formalism penetrated their *dîwâns*. Individuality, always in doubt and menaced by tradition in oriental literatures, becomes completely imperceptible from then on; lonely, bent upon his solitary labors, sometimes contradictory and vague, perhaps even deliberately so, and himself paying a very large tribute to tradition, the exceptional figure of Abû al-'Alâ' al-Ma'arrî (d. 1058) rises in this age of decadence.

The battle of the Abbasid period having ended in this way, medieval Arabic poetry was fossilized for centuries in the entire east. It is to the Maghrib, to North Africa and Spain, that the credit goes for introducing some new elements, which were both formal and conceptual, into this literary "unity" now grown terribly monotonous. Let us note, above all, how the lesson of the "Moderns," soon lost in the east under the dominant neoclassicism, seems to have left more lasting traces in the west, in a valuable Alexandrinism and fragmentarism, which is emphasized still more by the anthological collections (Ibn Bassâm, Ibn Khâqân, etc.) and which perpetuates in the west the new taste of Ibn al-Mu'tazz (d. 908), al-Ṣanawbarî, and others of the *muḥdathûn* of Iraq and of Syria. But beyond this more marked faithfulness to the "new school," the west brought two great innovations to medieval Arabic poetry: the strophic form and the use of the vulgar tongue, the *muwashshaḥa* and the *zajal,* which are a center of interest today for Arabic and Romance studies. The Andalusian origin of strophic poetry, whatever the uncertainty of names and dates for its beginnings, is at the same time affirmed by the whole Muslim historicoliterary tradition. Whatever may have been its possible but highly doubtful oriental precedents, the breaking-away by the Blind One of Qabra, or whoever it was, from the monorhymed scheme of the *qaṣîda,* and its articulation into the more supple strophic form with multiple rhymes, represented more than a purely metric novelty, and fresh blood began to run in the veins of the old poetry of the Arabian deserts. Opposed to the antique *qaṣîda* and its fixed scheme, there appeared not only the free erotic, descriptive, and bacchic *qiṭ'a* of the *muḥdathûn* but also a new type of composition which, in the play of its strophes, in its relaxation of the rules of classical poetry, and in its tendency to use the vulgar tongue, shortened the distance between art and life—a distance which had already been dangerously widened in Muslim society of the Middle Ages. The diffusion of the new art from the Maghrib, where it arose, once more stimulated the rapid and continuous circulation of Arabic culture; the extension of the vulgar tongue from the *kharja* (where according to the learned it had made its first appearance) to all of poetic composition, that is, the step from the *muwashshaḥa* in literary language to dialectical *zajal,* which was carried out we know not by whom or where (Ibn Quzmân [d. 1160] is the most important but neither the only one nor the first of the *zajjâlûn*), constitutes the most daring realistic effort in medieval Arabic poetry, with all the linguistic, literary, and social consequences which we are now in process of analyzing. This realistic attempt did not, however, succeed in breaking the domination of classical language and forms in the high literature of the Arabic-speaking world. As is demonstrated by many indications (Ibn Quzmân's *dîwân* copied in Palestine, the little treatise on the *muwashshaḥa* by Ibn Sanâ' al-Mulk, the attempts at *zajal* contained in the anthologies by the "orientals" al-Ḥillî and al-Ḥamawî), the Arabic east was highly interested in these Maghribî novelties but did not dare to develop them to the full, arrested as it was, at least so far as the *zajal* is concerned, by the prejudice against literary use of dialectical tongues. The valuable Andalusian innovation thus did not have anything like the revolutionary importance it might have had, that is, elevating to a literary level the Arabic dialects even outside the Maghrib. The divorce between cultivated literature and the spoken tongue was thus accentuated at the end of the Middle Ages and was imposed for good.

An examination of the evolution (or the involution) of Arabic prose leads us to similar conclusions, although it followed a different process. In the absence of literary usage in the pre-Islamic period, or at least of evidences which would demonstrate it, this prose at first attained a high prestige with the Koran and the oldest *ḥadîth* (which was historical and normative) and was spread over the whole of the Arabic world no less rapidly than was poetry. The Holy Book held a special position, naturally, whatever may have been the early and sacrilegious attempts at imitation. But the elaboration of profane prose by the Umayyad and Abbasid *kuttâb* created classical Arabic prose in the first two centuries of the hegira, with its principal center, like that of poetry, in Iraq: the prose of Ibn al-Muqaffa' (d. *ca.* 757), of al-Jâḥiẓ, of al-Tauḥîdî (d. 1023), and of al-Tanûkhî (d. 994), the sources of the *Aghânî* and of Ibn Qutaiba. As in the case of poetry of the classical type, it would be useless to seek any regional characteristics here, so great was the unity from the center to the periphery of this Arabo-Muslim culture, of this *adab* in the Arabic language which was open to influences from the great foreign cultures, Hellenistic, Iranian, and Indian. The great new formal innovation in Arabic prose cannot be traced back to local variations, but rather can be traced to the appearance in the ninth century of precious prose and its unfortunate victory in literary art. Modern Arab critics have sought to attribute this corruption of the simple, bold, and limber prose of the first two centuries to "Persian influence." Now it is well known that artificial prose was equally widespread, to the point of excess, in the Iranian literary domain; but it seems difficult to attribute the cause of the evil to Persia exclusively or in large part. It was actually an Arab, Ibn Duraid, to whom is attributed the origin of the *maqâma,* on account of his scenes of Bedouin life in the precious style; Arabs also, by blood and culture, were Ibn Nubâta (d. 984) and al-Khwârizmi (d. *ca.* 1000), al-Hamadhânî (d. 1008), and al-Ḥarîrî (d. 1122), those great virtuosos of the *saj‘,* who made a game and head-splitting exercise out of the literature of the *adab.* From Ibn Ḥayyân (d. 1076) to Ibn Bassâm (d. 1147), Arab also were all those western prose writers who produced in the new style, forcing into their rhythmic cadences and their word-plays the most interesting historical and literary material. Even if we admit some foreign influence as possible, we cannot fail to consider precious prose as a spontaneous degeneration of the innate Semitic tendency to parallelism and to rhythm, a tendency which was already present in the ancient *khuṭba,* sporadically and moderately employed by the great eighth and ninth-century prose writers, but overflowing in their successors to the point of drowning all content in verbal music. After the year 1000, only the new style of scientific, philosophic, and religious prose was saved from the contagion (and that not always), or the dry chronicle without pretensions to *adab;* but a literature of the *adab* which escaped the precious style is henceforth, from Mesopotamia to Andalusia, an exception. What is most surprising is the fact that the old style gave up without a struggle and without polemics, contrary to what happened in the battle of the old and the new poetry. It became the new fashion to attack the old style arrogantly (the scornful judgment of Hamadhânî of Jâḥiẓ as a writer is very significant here), but no counterblows came from the opposite camp. The very writer who did not succumb to the lure of the *saj'* felt neither the need nor even the possibility of expressly affirming his position, and no Arab rhetorician, so far as I know, opposed rhetorical excess from a theoretical standpoint. The diffusion of the most authentic product of the new style, the *maqâma,* not only in the whole Arabic linguistic territory but into the other Muslim (Persian and Turkish) literatures and even to non-Muslim neighbors (medieval Hebraic literature), gives the measure of the victory of a tendency which is so strange to us today but to which the most widely separated and varied minds of the Muslim Middle Ages gave their loyalty. If other phenomena point to the unity of "Arabic" culture, that of precious prose—although certainly Arabic in origin, as we see it—imposed itself, across the linguistic barriers, over the whole territory of Islâm.

Passing from form to content (which that form ended by practically destroying), we can isolate other more concrete influences in medieval Arabo-Islamic prose—influences which sometimes reveal local cultural aspects and currents. Such, in the west, are the traces of Hispanic epic and history, uncovered by Ribera in the most ancient Arabo-Spanish chroniclers, to which can be added those still more fragile traces, recently discovered by Levi Della Vida, of contacts between the Arabic culture in the west and the Latin culture of the low period (Orosius' histories). At the same time also, in Abbasid Iraq in the golden centuries, the stream of foreign cultures was spread through the translators and adapters from the Greek, the Syriac, the Pahlevi and, for the Indian world, through the solitary grandeur of al-Bêrûnî (d. 1048). But these cultural goods, transfused into the heart of the caliphate, rapidly became the common possessions of the whole Muslim world. Aristotle was studied by Avicenna in Persia as well as by Averroes in Morocco and in Spain, just as, in the realm of reading for entertainment, the *Kalîla and Dimna,* once it was introduced by Ibn al-Muqaffa' into Arabo-Muslim literature, traveled from one end of the *dâr al-Islâm* to the other, only to return to Persia wearing the inevitable dress of precious prose. But the work whose peregrinations perhaps show the unity and variety of medieval Arabic culture best is, as everyone knows, the *Thousand and One Nights.* A uniform Muslim patina has for centuries covered this classic of world literature, but, beneath this, modern criticism is able to perceive the various Arabic and non-Arabic layers in its immense material: first, traces of the Abbasid phase and more evident ones of the Egyptian phase which gave the celebrated collection its final outward form; while, from beyond the Arabic world, criticism also reveals evident traces of its distant Indian origin, and, still more surprising and suggestive, traces of the Hellenistic world, according to Von Grunebaum's recent studies. With these last might be associated not only the elements that have already been revealed in "The Voyages of Sindbad" but also a large group of love tales which recall, in the intrigue related, in their style, and in exposition, well-known models in the Alexandrian novel.

Arabic literature, in its centuries-long course and over the whole enormous territory through which it extended, was born from the reciprocal influence—sometimes harmonious, sometimes clashing—of two elements: a national, indigenous, and, although intellectually rudimentary, humanistic element, which was at the same time tight and exclusive in its racial pride; and a second, religious, international, universalist element, open because of these qualities to contacts and exchanges with other civilizations. The coexistence of these two elements in our opinion confers on Arabic literature all its breadth, the wide gamut of its interests, and its primacy within the world of Islâm, of which it was and remains the most direct and the most authoritative expression.

During the first two centuries of the hegira (practically until the middle of the ninth century A.D.) Islâm knew no literature other than the Arabic. The appearance about this time of neo-Persian literature is important not only for the history of Iran, which thus reaffirmed its national individuality, at least linguistically, but also for the whole Muslim civilization which with it begins to try out, alongside its mother-language, a new means of expression. The rapid and splendid blooming of this second Islamic literature is interesting, not only from a literary point of view, but also from the social and religious ones, for it breaks for the first time the close bond between Arabism and Islâm and opens new possibilities of spiritual affirmation to non-Arabic Muslim peoples. The well-known fact that the religious, juridical, and philosophic sciences for a long time continued to be treated in Arabic in Persia here remains secondary; what count are the literary and artistic means of expression, suited to expressing a different ethos, a national characteristic, a more than linguistic "variety" within the common Muslim culture. According to the terms of our problem, we can then ask the following question: What did neo-Persian literature bring to Islamic civilization that was new, what did it borrow, what did it prolong, what did it modify in Arabic literature, and what did it add that was original from its own ethnic and cultural background?

Persian literature's debt to the Arabic literature which preceded it and, so to speak, introduced it into the Islamic sphere certainly cannot be underestimated; to be convinced of this, it is only necessary to emphasize here the well-known linguistic phenomenon of the gradual and irresistible invasion of quite foreign structures into the Iranian language from the Arabic vocabulary and even from Arabic phraseology. To the linguistic integrity of the epic and, in less measure, of the oldest lyric poetry, to a certain abhorrence which the Persians at first had for gathering too many Arabic words into their tongue (an abhorrence which is shown to exist as late as the second half of the tenth century), there succeeded in the eleventh century the massive expansion within Persian of this Arabic vocabulary, which was to give and still gives its clearly composite character to that tongue. But it was not only a part of its lexicon that Arabic literature gave to Persia, but also literary kinds and rules, stylistic themes and models, metrics and rhetoric, a scientific and artistic terminology. Where the erotic and courtly lyric of the first stages is concerned, the most elementary chronological consideration obliges us to reverse the traditional thesis which explains the birth of the Arabic poetry of the Abbasid *muḥdathûn* by "Iranian influence" and to see in it, on the contrary, the model for the Persian poetry of the courts of Khurâsân and of Transoxania. Daudpota's study showed twenty years ago to what degree the poets at these courts followed the traditional Arabic models (the *nasîb,* in the first place, and sometimes even the archaic *nasîb* of Bedouin poetry), just as the images and concepts of the Abbasid *badî'* reappear, more or less happily copied in the new tongue. It is understood of course that, once neo-Persian literature was established, the influence became reciprocal within a culture that was often bilingual, a fact which did not prevent the first models from being offered by the already mature Arabic art to the just emerging neo-Persian literature. At the same time, even in this realm, Persian literature certainly did not restrict itself to slavish imitation and immediately introduced novelties in form and content (the creation of the autonomous *ghazal* following detachment of the traditional *nasîb* from the rest of the *qaṣîda,* of the *rubâ'î* which was destined to receive the eternal imprint of Iranian genius, and of the *mathnavî* immediately consecrated by the epic), just as Persian literature infused new life into even the most commonplace elements (the bacchic theme and the gnomic-pessimistic theme, both brought to a high perfection by Khayyâm), thanks to the splendor of a rapidly stylized repertory of images and to a language which reached no less rapidly an unmatchable fluidity and harmony.

And yet it is not in lyric, courtly, and erotic poetry that Muslim Persia made its most original contribution to world literature but, as everyone knows, in the heroic and romantic epic. The Arabic muse which had inspired it elsewhere failed it here, and the Iranian spirit really drew upon its own resources and created absolutely original works which did not depend in the least on the patterns and products of the elder literature of Islâm. Even if we abstain here from any aesthetic appreciation of the writers, we cannot fail to recognize in Firdausî (d. *ca.* 1020) and Niẓâmî (d. 1203) the most eloquent spokesmen of the national tradition in their poems, which became perfect models for Persian literature and for all those who were inspired by it in this respect. With the heroic and knightly *mathnavî,* Iran produced an indubitably original note in the orchestra of Muslim literature. Only an abstract consideration of content, however, can fail to see in Niẓâmî and Firdausî the links that join them to medieval Muslim civilization, which they were both dependent upon and which is more or less clearly revealed in their works. The *Shâh-Nâma* has been called by turns pagan and Zoroastrian, foreign to Islâm; and certainly its matter is quite extra-Islamic and the poet's emotional adherence to the heroic and distant world he celebrates very sincere. Nonetheless, it remains true that the social and cultural reality of an already Islamized Iran sometimes shines through even the archaic Firdausian poem and does so even more in Niẓâmî's various exquisite romantic poems, all impregnated, although to different degrees, by Muslim culture and piety, as anyone must be aware who has truly read the *Khamsa* in the original. These remarks, brief as they are, are intended as a reaction against the tendency which certain historians of Persian literature have shown (and I must recall here the illustrious name of my compatriot Italo Pizzi) to detach the epic and the romantic Persian poets from the social and religious atmosphere that surrounded them—to make them, as it were, champions of an "Aryan" tradition which, if it ever existed in a pure form in Persia, perished at the same time as did the Sassanid state and civilization. Islâm's imprint, once made upon a people, is never effaced, and the great Persian poets, even when they treat material anterior and exterior to Islâm, carry its stamp no less.

Persian literature was to make a still more direct and fecund contribution to Islamic spirituality with its mystic poetry when it vied in this field, according to its own genius, with Arabic literature and soon exceeded it by its inventive talent and its variety of exposition, perhaps even by its speculative depth. Lyric poetry, the apologue, and mystic meditation constitute the field in which the two great Islamic literatures took one another's measure, and the palm goes without any contest to Iranian literature. Ṣûfism, born in the Arabic world and counting its theoreticians, visionaries, and saints among the Arabs by the hundreds, never succeeded in expressing itself in Arabic except by an abstruse and turgid so-called "lyric," if we make an exception for the few but unforgettable verses of al-Ḥallâj (d. 922), and by a very rich ascetic output of only moderate literary worth. The Persian genius alone gave to Muslim mysticism the glory of a luxuriant poetic bloom in which the innate aptitude of the Iranians for narration and the sentence combined with the energy of a highly stimulated emotionality and with the audacity of the most unbridled esoteric speculations. It is from this that there came, again without equivalents in Arabic literature, the poems of Rûmî (d. 1273), of 'Aṭṭâr (d. *ca.* 1230), and of Jâmî (d. 1492), the religious outpourings of Abû Sa'îd (d. 1049) and of Rûmî himself, the refined gnomicolyric embroideries of Sa'dî (d. 1291) and of Ḥâfiz (d. *ca.* 1390)—the most brilliant pleiad in the Persian poetic firmament. The voice of Islamic Ṣûfism seems far more appealing in the works of these Persians than in the very vast asceticomystic Arab literature, which goes from the austere sentences of Ḥasan al-Baṣrî to the obscure *qaṣîdas* of Ibn al-Fâriḍ; and all the great minds of the West, from Goethe to Hegel, who sought to approach this aspect of Muslim spirituality, actually took as their guides not the Arabic ascetics or doctors but the great Persian poets we have just named.

As recompense, if it was one, for this contribution to the religious poetry of Islâm, Persian literature received from Arabic literature during these centuries, if what we have suggested about the origin of precious prose is correct, the seeds of degeneration of its prose style. Surely the Iranian literary genius must have been predisposed to the malady, so easily did the disease capture it, spoiling the vigor and freshness of the prose of its beginnings and reducing it to that hybrid, undigested mixture from which only the contemporary period has begun to liberate itself—and that, not without some difficulty. For lack of space we must restrict ourselves to this comment. In concluding these few observations on what Persia brought to Islamic culture during the classical period, it seems to us that this can be defined by certain original aspects in profane literary creations (epic and narrative) and by the intensity and the brilliant color of religious expression (Ṣûfî poetry). We might also recall, in a field involving prose but one more scientific than literary, the work of the great historians of the Mongol period, which surpasses by far the Arabic historiography of the same centuries.

For obvious geographical and linguistic reasons Persian literature remained foreign to western Islâm, while from the beginning of the thirteenth century it began to fertilize the spiritual life of the Islamic peoples east of the Mediterranean. Three ethnic groups underwent the religious and cultural influence of Islâm through Persia as intermediary: the Hindus, Mongols, and Turks. It is only among the last named, however (leaving aside the not very important Hindustani literature), that the Persian influence manifested itself in their own national language or languages. The group of Turkish Islamic literatures, primarily the Chaghatai and the Osmanli, depends much more closely on the Persian model than Persian literature had ever depended on the Arabic; these literatures, indeed, add nothing to their model that is new in either spirit or form, while we have seen the importance of what Persia brought to the literary patrimony of Islâm. True, the Turks also possessed a crude and strong folklore of their own, which they brought along with them on their migrations from the heart of Central Asia; but this pre-Islamic background, in contrast to those of the Arabs and of the Persians, was almost totally abandoned by the Islamized Turks, who were immediately attracted by the two great full-grown and refined Muslim literatures, especially the Persian. The few surviving monuments of Turkish epic and national folklore, like the recently restudied *Dede Qorqut,* clash sharply with the customary background of Islamized Turkish literature. The latter, from its first efforts (the *Qudatqu Bilik* of the eleventh century and the other minor writings belonging to the period and the environment of the Qarakhânids of Central Asia), leaned directly upon Iranian models—on the "Mirrors for Princes" and the treatises on government of the Seljuq epoch—thus already taking on its character as a courtly, conventional, and imitative art. The same is true for the whole Chaghatai literature (which culminates at the end of the fifteenth century with Nevâ'î at the court of the Tîmûrids) and for a good portion of the Osmanli literature, which appeared in Seljuq Anatolia in the thirteenth century and was carried on, with Istanbul as its center, until the crisis of the last century. Admirers of literature conceived as the authentic expression of the soul of a people, of those *Stimmen der Völker* which appear also in Arabic and Persian literature although narrowed into the most rigid stylization, are likely to regret that such voices were so rapidly killed in Turkish literature, stifled as they were by the cold artistic literature—by that *divan edebiyatı* which today's Turks regard with boredom and scorn. The spontaneous popular current which, with Sultan Veled (d. 1312), Yunus Emre (first half of fourteenth century) and the other older poets, took a spark from the great fire of Persian mysticism and caused it to glow in simple and innocent forms in their national tongue, was quickly extinguished before the artificial current which dominated Ottoman literature for four centuries. The pattern of the Persian poetic world is stamped upon it to the point of the most exhausting monotony, from romantic poems in the manner of Niẓâmî to the courtly and aristocratic poetry, as well as to the burlesque satires where, at the most, one may find some few happy touches of realism. This whole "literature," in the worst sense of the word, follows the rising and then falling curve of the last Muslim empire and collapses, with that state's medieval structure, during the nineteenth century. It is not by chance that, of the three master literatures of Islâm, Turkish literature was the first to go into a crisis upon contact with the West and to move forward daringly and even radically on the way to a total remodeling. This most artificial organism, bred upon foreign models and values, fell almost without any resistance under the innovating shock of European thought and art.

The modern and contemporary phase of Muslim literatures is outside the limits which we have set ourselves in this article, which had for its object summarily to touch upon the principal currents and contrasts; it is outside our scope for the very reason that the modern period saw the weakening of the common denominator of the Muslim civilizations, against the background of which we have seen the three master literatures by which this civilization was expressed, bound to each other in a chain, so to speak. In the years closest to us, as the religious bond has been relaxed and the *dâr al-Islâm* has dissolved into touchy nationalisms (whatever may be the federalist efforts of the type of the Arab League), Islâm's unity was broken up, even in the literary realm; each of these literatures, indeed, reacted in a different way to the preponderant influence of the West, seeking to conciliate it or to repudiate ancient values in its favor. But this concerns history in process, while our analysis is devoted to history which took place long ago.

If we may make one last observation, which joins the past to the present of the three Muslim literatures, we cannot fail to remark on the differing fates of their respective languages. In Persia and in Turkey the national languages, even when they were in the past twisted into a very rigorous literary stylization, kept their character as living languages, and the spontaneous inclinations of many modern writers, sometimes helped and sometimes hindered by governmental undertakings to "purify" the language, have little by little filled in the gap between the written and the spoken tongue. In all the Arab countries, on the other hand, as everyone knows, the general phenomenon of the split between written and spoken language long ago ended in bilingualism. We cannot elaborate here the complex problems of a literary, political, and social order that this duality raises in the modern Arab world. We must, however, notice that this Arabic bilingualism has reversed the relation existing between literature and life, as it marked the three Muslim literatures at their start and for some time. Arabic literature, in which at the outset this relationship was the closest and the most fruitful (one need only think of the origins of Islâm, of the whole Umayyad period, of the golden age of the Abbasid caliphate), has seen this gap widen, as a result of bilingualism, to the point of the disconcerting hiatus in modern times, which the more lively contemporary forces are trying, more or less successfully, to fill. The Persian and Turkish literatures, on the contrary, although courtly and aristocratic from their birth, and expressions of social and intellectual elites, have, because of the single fact of having maintained the substantial unity of the linguistic instrument, been able—first in the case of the Turkish and, recently and more slowly, of the Persian—to go toward the people, to turn to their needs and interests, without in the process breaking all continuity with the national literary tradition. Whatever the position of each of us may be on the theoretical problems of language, we cannot fail to appreciate the enormous literary and social importance of such differing situations among the different Muslim nations. This is the latest case of variety in the long-wavering unity of the old *dâr al-Islâm,* a variety which our statement could not pass over in silence.